READERS THEATRE

READERS THEATRE

What it is and
  How to Stage it
    by Marvin Kaye

with a Preface
    by Mary Stuart

and

Four Award-Winning Scripts by
    Charles LaBorde
        Jo Davidsmeyer
            Caroline E. Wood
                Robert Hawkins

WILDSIDE PRESS

NEWARK, NJ ● 1995

822
56530

READERS THEATRE

The support and assistance of many persons made this anthology possible. Especial thanks are due Carol Higgins Clark, Edmee Firth, executive director of the Jean And Louis Dreyfus Foundation; Beth Goehring, editorial director of The Fireside Theatre; John Jakes, Fulton Macdonald, adjunct assistant professor at New York University; Rex Robbins, Mary Stuart, Nancy Temple, charter member and public relations director of The Open Book and George White, founder and president of the Eugene O'Neill National Theater Center and the National Playwrighting Competition in Waterford, Connecticut.

ISBN: 1-880448-49-1

CONTENTS

To
Professor Fulton Macdonald
of New York University
who spurred us to create
a readers theatre playwrighting competition
and to
Isidor Weingarten
for coming to every production
of The Open Book
since 1976

PREFACE

For me, the most exciting part of being involved with the First National Readers Theatre Competition was discovering how much good, really original, truly wonderful theatre is being written in every part of the country.

Ninety-five scripts were submitted to this competition and among them were some extraordinary plays. I was only privileged to read those selected as finalists, of which four are included in this book, but as you will see, they present a real cross section of subjects, character and style, and they are all important.

The first place winner, *Memorial* by Charles LaBorde, is an amazingly powerful play. A continual barrage of short scenes, unforgettable images and moments on what is probably a bare stage create a mosaic that makes the war in Vietnam and the men and women who fought it devastatingly real. The first runner-up, *Angel* by Jo Davidsmeyer, is described as "A Nightmare of the Holocaust." Ms Davidsmeyer makes the nightmare your own, but somehow she also makes it possible to handle the horror intellectually. The second runner-up, *The Immigrant Garden* by Caroline E. Wood, has a gentle tenderness that will haunt you. Finally, the fourth runner-up, *Quiet! Three Ladies Laughing* by Robert Hawkins, has wit and a nostalgia that are at once reassuring and very disquieting.

Writing a play is hard work, and everybody knows that. It is also lonely work and it takes incredible drive, skill and patience to see a play to the final curtain. Writing a good play takes rare gifts of talent, insight and sensitivity. So we must be very grateful to the playwrights who have chosen this labor of love. We all need a mirror of ourselves and our society. We desperately need a chance to see our world from another point of view, another perspective. We also know that, historically, the theatre has always been the best place to find it.

Applause! Applause! then for the brilliantly talented people who have offered us so much of themselves. Applause! Applause! Congratulations and many, many thanks.

—Mary Stuart
New York City, 1995

INTRODUCTION

The story of the First National Readers Theatre Playwrighting Competition has two beginnings.

In 1975, a group of professional actors, writers, educators and singers—Bill Bonham, Beverly Fite, Parke Godwin, Saralee Kaye, June Miller, Toby Sanders, Nancy Temple and myself—created The Open Book, New York City's first professional readers theatre ensemble.

The purpose of The Open Book was and is to present a wide variety of worthwhile literature not currently familiar to the public; to stimulate public interest in such literature by oral interpretation in a novel, comprehensible format; to commission new works suitable for readers theatre with particular emphasis on meritorious authors and projects unlikely to be produced by other theatre companies.

The Open Book devised a unique performing style based on elements of traditional acting combined with methods drawn from oral interpretation and readers theatre, plus antiphonal devices such as the controlled dynamics and multiple rhythms generally associated with chamber or choral music (what I call "The Open Book effect.")

The ensemble became a tax-free nonprofit company in 1980. For fifteen years, it performed at several venues, including twice-a-year appearances at Lincoln Center, as well as Barnes & Noble bookstores, the Magic Towne House and Symphony Space. A widely varied repertoire reflected The Open Book's official motto, "the best of all worlds of literature" —from dramas old and new through theatrically-arranged prose and a pyrotechnic anthology of poems and songs, *Poetry in Motion*, The Open Book's "signature piece" that has played to enthusiastic New York audiences, as well as at the Folger Shakespeare Theatre in Washington, D. C. One of the company's most unusual productions was *Bertrand Russell's* Guided Tour of Intellectual Rubbish, the only dramatization of Lord Russell's life and writings to be approved by the Russell estate, his publishers and the Bertrand Russell Peace Foundation.

In 1990, The Open Book moved to the Amsterdam Room, a nonconventional performing space on Manhattan's West Side, where the company specializes in a "living room" brand of intimate theatre that in five seasons has included such varied fare as the American premiere of Gerald Moon (*Corpse*) and Marianne McNaghten's Romanoff tragedy, *Dearest Nicky, Darling Alex*; the Plautus farce *Assinine*; an *a cappella* musical version of Daniel Pinkwater's popular children's book, *The Hoboken Chicken Emergency*;

a tongue-in-cheek collection of Hallowe'en horror stories and songs, *The Lighter Side of Darkness*, and the four superb scripts featured in this collection.

Beginning Number Two . . .

As adjunct professor of creative writing at New York University, I am permitted to audit courses in the School of Continuing Education. For several years I have "sat in" on excellent classes at NYU devoted to sound business practice. The most valuable of these courses was Professor Fulton Macdonald's Public and Private Partnerships, a relatively new fundraising concept designed to aid nonprofit organizations in seeking and obtaining corporate assistance.

Fulfilling a homework assignment, I wrote a proposal to Beth Goehring, editor-in-chief of The Fireside Theatre, to conduct with The Open Book a national playwrighting competition that would help develop awareness amongst professional actors, agents, critics, directors, producers and writers that readers theatre *has little to do with "staged readings,"* but is, instead, a distinct and distinctive, comparatively economical system for restoring creative imagination to the ailing American theatre.

Beth's sunny encouragement, advice and emotional support made both the First National Readers Theatre Playwrighting Competition and this anthology possible. Wildside Press publisher John Betancourt also deserves thanks for possessing the creative vision and cultural literacy that helped make this labor of love a reality. Thanks, too, to the judges who helped choose these four scripts from a field of approximately one hundred submissions: Carol Higgins Clark, John Jakes, Rex Robbins and Mary Stuart.

To fully analyze the principles of script adaptation and directing involved in readers theatre would require an entire book, and the four winning scripts are the true stars of this collection. In the opening chapter, I have restricted myself to defining readers theatre, while the second chapter discusses some of the staging techniques devised at The Open Book to produce "the best of all worlds of literature."

As I write this introduction, the second annual playwrighting competition is in full swing, and by the time this book is published, the third competition will be in its early stages. Script submission information is provided in Appendix I.

—Marvin Kaye
Artistic Director, The Open Book
November 1994, New York City

WHAT *IS* READER'S THEATRE?

One afternoon last August, Beverly Fite, a charter member of The Open Book, was riding the subway on her way to a rehearsal of Caroline E. Wood's play in the form of letters, *The Immigrant Garden*, when she noticed that one of her fellow passengers was reading the script over her shoulder and had tears in her eyes.

B ("My friends call me B. Not B-E-A, just B") introduced herself and discovered her travel companion was another theatre person, Bobbie Hellard, of Ramona, California. Bobbie began to apologize for peeking at B's mail, only to find out that the passage she'd read was actually part of a new play.

"How fortunate you are to be working on such a touching script," Ms Hellard later wrote. "In this day where words assault and offend, your lines are like the lavender-scented breeze. It never ceases to amaze me that all of the high-tech special effects people hunger for these days cannot measure up to *the power of well-chosen words*."

That phrase embodies the essence of readers theatre. Critic Walter Kerr once observed in a review of a production of Büchner's *Danton's Death* that despite the milling throngs and undeniably exciting spectacle, the drama— and by extension, *all* drama—does not get under way till the crowds exit and Danton confronts Robespierre, one on one. Which is another way of saying that mise en scene is a poor substitute for the power of language. Elaborate costumes, lighting effects, settings, even mime and dance are the baggage of Hellmouth.

Bill Bonham, cofounder and president of The Open Book, defines readers theatre as "a creative, fluid art form that presents all styles of literature, focusing on the experience found in the writer's text and encouraging the active imagination and intellectual participation of the audience. It is a presentational form, suggesting rather than representing the literature's physical elements. Thus, one reader may assume multiple roles, two or more readers may play one character, and minimal settings, costumes and lighting are fleshed out in the minds of the spectators. It is often referred to as 'theatre of the mind.' A member of our audience once called it 'visual radio.' "

The two key elements of this definition are presentationalism and textual illumination.

In John Gassner's *Producing the Play*, Mordecai Gorelik defines presentationalism as "staging which emphasizes . . . a direct relationship between the performers and the audience. Presentational staging removes that invisible 'fourth wall' which remains in (representational) staging even after the curtain is lifted."

In traditional theatre, presentationalism is generally associated with those asides and soliloquies commonly found in Shakespeare, Marlowe, Goldoni, Moliere, commedia dell'arte, Restoration comedy, etc. In readers theatre, however, direct eye contact is made often with audience members. Actors who appear with The Open Book are told that when there is an invisible "fourth wall," it is only waist-high and must be peeped over from time to time.1

Most actors admit the necessity of illuminating the author's text, but too often that only implies the motivational study of "beats" and "actions" associated with Stanislavski's method of physical objectives. In readers theatre, texts must be analyzed, adapted and orchestrated with the meticulous attention to detail that the members of a string quartet bring to every measure and note of the music they plan to interpret. The texture, sonority and tessitura of the human voice is applied to the author's denotations, gradations and connotations in order to stir in the audience's collective imagination a verbal (and sometimes literal) music of meaning and emotion far more potent than moods cast on painted flats by gel-covered Lekos.

By now, it should be evident that readers theatre has little in common with "staged readings." The word "readers" is probably responsible for the error, similar to how Physician Assistants are sometimes confused with nurses instead of being recognized as the case-managing medical professionals they actually are.

The physical scripts sometimes seen onstage in readers theatre productions are purely symbolic. In The Open Book, performers are required to memorize their lines, and often the books are only seen at the beginning and end of a performance. (The final curtain call is always reserved for the script itself).

*   *   *

In America, the origin of readers theatre is generally attributed to

---

1   The ensuing chapter discusses this convention's aesthetic basis.

developments in the speech and oral interpretation curriculum at North-western University and other schools. Directors, educators and writers like Leslie Irene Coger, Harriet Nesbit, Shirlee Sloyer, Melvin R. White, Judy E. Yordon and many others explored techniques and forms of analysis and interpretation, some of which are examined in the next chapter. In a broader sense, however, readers theatre shares a common heritage with traditional theatre. In an article in the June 1932 issue of the *Quarterly Journal of Speech*, Eugene Bahn traces the beginnings of interpretive reading (from which readers theatre derives) to that moment in the early Greek drama when the actor playing Thespis stepped forward to tell the audience a narrative myth. This is the same moment of choral delineation that theatrical scholars point to when asked to trace the rise of the modern stage.

Coupled with the fact that certain readers theatre performance techniques are analogous to bygone dramatic practice, this common origin suggests that readers theatre is not a new art form, but an old one which speech and oral interpretation professors have rescued and refurbished.

In the past several years, a number of popular plays and musicals have profitably employed readers theatre techniques, sometimes intentionally (*The Grapes of Wrath*), sometimes serendipitously (*Nicholas Nickleby*). It is high time that more performing artists discovered the strengths and advantages of this pyrotechnic, yet relatively economical art form.

SUGGESTIONS FOR STAGING READERS THEATRE

In the twenty years that The Open Book has been in existence, I have often been asked to explain the difference between staging readers theatre and directing any show in an intimate, minimalist style. Perhaps an oral interpretation expert's answer to this question might differ from that of a traditional theatre artist, but that is just another way of saying that Freud's patients have Freudian dreams while Jung's are Jungian. The methods vary; the goal does not.

The main difference is that readers theatre employs a distinctive set of interpretive tools to foreshorten the empathetic distance between the script (and performers) and the audience. Some traditional theatrical elements are minimized or eliminated, but this simplicity of presentation is an aesthetic, not budgetary, choice. Unlike a staged reading, readers theatre is not merely a way station in the development of a new play, but is an alternative performance technique, complete unto itself. Cumbersome scenery, elaborate costumes, makeup and special lighting effects are more or less replaced by elements of presentationalism and sophisticated textual analysis that jointly aim to focus the audience's imagination on the imagery and sonority contained within the writer's text.

The present chapter is a practical introduction to some of the basic techniques of readers theatre staging.

SCRIPT SELECTION AND ADAPTATION

Selecting and adapting literature for readers theatre is too extensive to cover adequately in a single chapter, but we can offer a brief overview of the topic, mixed with a bit of practical advice.

Theoretically, all literature can be adapted to suit the form's performance characteristics. Poetry can be effectively arranged for solo, group and/or choral reading. Narrative fiction can be dramatized in a variety of readers theatre performance styles. One useful method, which some (though not all) readers theatre experts call *chamber theatre*, is similar to traditional theatre insofar as the actors are each responsible for a single character. But they not only speak the dialogue, but also the descriptive passages pertinent to her or his character. In my adaptation of Daniel Pinkwater's humorous fantasy, *Blue Moose*, two performers play a French chef named Mr. Breton and the titular moose. Here is an brief example from this chamber theatre script:

THE MOOSE

Do you mind if I come in and get warm? I'm just about frozen.

(to the audience)

The moose brushed past him and walked into the kitchen. His antlers almost touched the ceiling. The moose sat down on the floor—

MR. BRETON

—next to Mr. Breton's stove.

THE MOOSE

The moose didn't move. Wisps of steam began to rise from his blue fur. After a long time the moose sighed . . .

(Loud sigh)

MR. BRETON

He sounded like a foghorn.

(He addresses the moose)

Can I get you a cup of coffee? Or some clam chowder?

Some readers theatre writers consider nonfiction inappropriate for adaptation, yet factual material has been handled effectively in a number of shows that contain elements of readers theatre—for instance, Samuel Gallu's *Give 'em Hell, Harry*; Fredd Wayne's *Ben Franklin, Gentleman*, or Douglas Scott's *Mountain*, in which Len Cariou portrayed Chief Justice William O. Douglas while Heather Summerhayes and John C. Vennema played everyone else. One of The Open Book's most interesting shows is *Bertrand Russell's Guided Tour of Intellectual Rubbish*, a "platform lecture" with dramatic interludes devised from approximately two dozen of Lord Russell's books on education, philosophy, politics, science and sex.

Some playwrighting contests refuse adaptations, but the ability to fashion a dramatic event from narrative prose, poetry or nonfiction is one of readers theatre's strongest virtues, so The Open Book and The Fireside Theatre competition decided to accept adaptations. Those received describe a broad artistic spectrum from slapdash butcherings of various literary compositions to brilliantly-conceived scripts drawn from the lives and works of authors, generals, holocaust survivors, musicians, politicians and social reformers.

What this proves is that a good readers theatre adaptation is more than a cut-and-paste job. Charles LaBorde's script, *Memorial*, is largely derived from interviews he conducted with Vietnam veterans, but he was not content to distribute his dialogue to actors sitting on stools with spotlights jumping from one to the other as they take turns speaking. The playwright's remarkable theatricalization of his raw material is what makes *Memorial* a masterful composition.

Paradoxically, dramatic literature is the most problematic literary form to adapt. While it is theoretically possible to produce any play in readers theatre format, I believe that a medium that is essentially minimalistic precludes choosing plays that depend for their effectiveness on elaborate lighting or sets. At staged readings, the stage directions are assigned to a narrator, an option that is always available in readers theatre—but not always effective. A play rooted in character like Robert Hawkins's *Quiet! Three Ladies Laughing* might benefit from a minimalist approach, but the substitution of a narrator for the awesome set and harrowing scenic effects required in Patrick Meyers's *K2* would be intolerable.

CASTING

Readers theatre performers must have flexible, versatile voices and be completely comfortable making direct eye contact with the audience. Of approximately 1,200 professional resumés that The Open Book received in the past two years, fewer than one hundred applicants possessed these necessary skills. Anticipating this very problem two decades ago, our charter members devoted an entire year to rehearsing all literary forms—prose, poetry, drama, even nonfiction—so that the ensemble virtually became one actor with six voices. As new members were added, they learned from the original six and in turn became mentors for the next set of jobbers, thus providing a system of artistic continuity.

Obviously, creating an ensemble in this fashion is artistically demanding and time-consuming. Since most producers do not have the option of training each new set of actors from scratch, a few words of advice concerning readers theatre casting may be helpful.

Actors grounded in both solo oral interpretation and ensemble readers theatre are in comparatively short supply in New York City, but certain other performers tend to adapt well to the form—cabaret and concert singers, Shakespearean and classically-trained actors and also professional comedy improvisers, especially those who have worked with the methods in Keith Johnstone's seminal textbook, *Impro*. All three of these disciplines groom practitioners in two key readers theatre skills, textual analysis2 and presentationalism.

At Open Book auditions, two factors weigh heavily. The first is the ability to "cold read" difficult literature. We assign on-the-spot passages from Dickens, Shakespeare and such other language-rich authors as Matthew Arnold, James M. Barrie, Ray Bradbury, Edna Ferber, Bernard Shaw, Sara Teasdale, Dylan Thomas . . . to name just a few.

Previously prepared monologues tell little about a performer's basal ability because there is no way of knowing how much advance preparation and outside direction contributed to the end result. "Cold reading," on the other hand, reveals the prospective jobber's precise irreducible level of skill. Does he stumble over diction and syntax, or is he able at first sight to effectively handle various literary styles and vocabularies? Can he meaningfully interpret several lines of blank verse on a single breath without rushing?

The second factor we evaluate is more subjective in nature, a phenomenon speech teachers refer to as "personal proof." This is just a fancy label for that quality an actor projects upon her or his first entrance. Because readers theatre performers must interact personably with the patrons, one's initial reaction to an auditioner may be a vital indicator of how the audience will respond to her or him.

Readers theatre is well suited to doubling and countercasting. Women can play men, adults can substitute for children, young for old; one actor may appear in several roles. But the use of multiple casting should not be solely to save money. The governing principle should be: how many performers does this script require to do it justice?

PRESENTATIONALISM: WHAT, WHY & HOW

The trend in western theatre this century has been away from fourth-wall realism. Besides those experiments in alienation and objectification associated with Bertolt Brecht and the Absurdists, presentationalism has been explored by such writers as Edward Albee, David Edgar, T. S. Eliot, Joseph Heller, Arthur Kopit, Percy MacKaye, Archibald MacLeish, Arthur Miller, Eugene O'Neill, Douglas Scott, Neil Simon, Thornton Wilder, both Emlyn and Tennessee Williams—the list is far from complete.

Presentational devices employed by these and other writers include asides and/or soliloquies; use of a narrator or "Greek chorus"; scenes of action that take place outside the proscenium arch, sometimes virtually in

---

2   Though improvisers create their own texts, to gain proficiency they
     must study and thoroughly assimilate narrative structure.

the laps of the audience; use of the theatre as the actual location of the drama; recognition of the presence of the spectators, often combined with assignment of a collective identity to them (the audience as dissidents: Clifford Odets's *Waiting for Lefty*; as jury: Ayn Rand's *Night of January 16th* or Robert Shaw's *The Man in the Glass Booth*; as unwitting conspirators: Rupert Holmes's *Accomplice*; as potential victims: Joseph Dolan Tuotti's *Big Time Buck White*.) Such highly theatrical methods enable playwrights to achieve effects outside the usual scope of fourth-wall representationalism. Viewed from a traditional perspective, one might reasonably argue that presentationalism is not universal, but exists on a case-by-case basis.3 But in readers theatre, though the extent of audience interaction varies from show to show, some degree of presentationalism is *always* present. This is because one of the cast's main goals is to involve the spectators in a shared literary experience. When an Open Book production employs an invisible fourth wall, the performers are reminded that it is only waist-high. From time to time, they are instructed to peep over it and reestablish direct eye contact with the audience.

This feature of readers theatre consistently troubles actors untrained in presentational methods, yet even those experienced in playing the asides and soliloquies of, say, Shakespeare or Moliere may be disconcerted to learn that in readers theatre they are never permitted to vanish completely into their characters. Rather, each appears as *a formalized version of her- or himself, an intermediary between the literature and the audience.*

At the beginning of every Open Book show, the cast (or a portion of the cast) enters and smiles at the audience with this distinct subtext: "We want to share a book (or play or poem) with you. We love it, and we hope you will, too." If the spectators immediately like the performers, they are more apt to participate actively in the planned literary experience. Like "golden age" radio, readers theatre is an art that, in order to succeed, must actively involve the audience's imagination.

Thus, the director must assess each script for various kinds of opportunities to engage the viewers in this collaborative creative process. This assessment might be obvious, as in Charles LaBorde's *Memorial*, most of which is obviously meant to be spoken directly to the audience, or in the

---

3   In *The Monologue Workshop*, Jack Poggi implies that, historically, presentationalism may be the theatrical "norm," with fourth-wall representationalism merely a passé byproduct of naturalism.

opening scene of Jo Davidsmeyer's *Angel*, where Irma Grese addresses the crowd as if it had just arrived at Auschwitz. More often, though, presentational moments have to be specially devised, as, for instance, in our production of Caroline E. Wood's *The Immigrant Garden* when Mrs. Beauchamp was directed to deliver several of her epistolary bon mots directly to the audience.

Depending on the nature of the show, readers theatre performers may fulfill any or all of the following four presentational tasks:

1. *Personal proof*: The first actors to appear are responsible for establishing rapport with the audience.

2. *Introductory*: Often, the performers must set the mood and introduce the literature. There are many ways to do this. Perhaps the show is a dramatized work of fiction (or even nonfiction) that introduces itself, as, for example, Charles Dickens's *A Tale of Two Cities*: "It was the best of times, it was the worst of times—" If it is a play by Bernard Shaw, one might wish to adapt (and probably abridge) the author's own prefatory remarks.4 An excellent technique is to invite the performers to write and speak their own introduction(s). Challenging the cast to verbalize its personal attitude toward the literature is quintessential readers theatre.

3. *Ongoing narration*: In a show structured like a review, as, for instance, The Open Book's verse anthology, *Poetry in Motion*, the actors simply appear as formalized versions of themselves. Each new selection is introduced by the performers, and eye contact with the audience is frequent and ongoing. But when staging a play in readers theatre, do not assign a narrator to read all of the stage directions. Good playwrighting, combined with a synopsis of scenes in the printed program, should be sufficient to set the scene for the audience. There is only one valid reason for employing a narrator between scenes of a play performed in readers theatre, and that is to reestablish the presentational connection with the audience, as in The Open Book's staging of Bob Hawkins's *Quiet! Three Ladies Laughing*, in which the same actor played both Lou Berta and Diedre and also served as narrator. At the beginning of the show, she announced the title and author, then delivered a *condensed* version of the first stage direction: "The scene is a sleeping porch at the Nolan homeplace in north Alabama during 1943. It

---

4   Presuming permission is obtainable from the dramatist's estate and
     publishers. *Be careful*. Permission to perform a published
     play generally does not automatically include prefatory material.

is early afternoon and the sun is shining through the shutters. Lou Berta, the family maid, surveys the scene, shaking her head in disbelief." The actor then "became" Lou Berta, whose opening lines dovetail with her function as narrator/Greek chorus. From time to time, she reappeared as the narrator. For instance, at the beginning of Act Two, Scene Three, she told the audience, "Our story ends later that day, out on the front porch. Miss Lula's funeral has come and gone, and the Nolans are all back from the cemetery."

4. *Asides to the audience*: In an anthology show, where the performers basically appear as themselves, eye contact is a vital part of the form, but even in a "fourth wall" show, the presentational nature of readers theatre permits actors to speak directly to individual audience members. The asides and soliloquies associated with Moliere, Shakespeare and their contemporaries are obvious candidates for this technique, but any universalized sentiment is fair game for a remark to the audience. In The Open Book's production of Chekhov's *The Boor*, for example, the actors playing Smirnoff and Madame Popova each peeped over the aforementioned waist-high fourth wall to rail against the opposite sex by singling out and haranguing hapless distaff and masculine patrons. Similarly, one may profitably adapt prefatory remarks, afterwords or footnotes (provided, of course, that permission has been obtained.) In The Open Book's production of James M. Barrie's great proto-feminist play, *The Twelve-Pound Look*, a narrator sitting off to one side from time to time shared with the audience the playwright's witty comments to the reader.

TEXTUAL ANALYSIS

In any production situation, the first responsibility of the director and cast is to study the text. What is the writer trying to say? How does the work's prevailing mood, or sequence of moods, contribute to the author's overall intent? Once the text has been thoroughly analyzed, the artists begin to make choices on how to interpret it. A director may make a flow chart of the script's motivational units. The actors may dissect their characters in terms of Stanislavskian "beats" and "objectives." This is all as it should be, but in readers theatre, textual analysis is even more complicated. Furthermore, disparate tasks confront the actor and the director.

1. *The actor's textual analysis*: Modern readers theatre is an outgrowth of the oral interpretation programs at various university speech departments. Students performing all modes of literature, not just dramatic, have devised methods of marking scripts for rhythmic patterns and rate of delivery, dynamics and timbre, inflectional and tonal variety or, as I prefer to think of it, orchestration. An experienced performer may virtually "score" the

script like music.

The complexity of the technique involved can be demonstrated by analyzing two excerpts from Charles Dickens's novel, *Bleak House*.

First, let us examine its opening paragraph:

London. Michaelmas term lately over, and the Lord Chancellor sitting in Lincoln's Inn Hall. Implacable November weather. As much mud in the streets as if the waters had but newly retired from the face of the earth, and it would not be wonderful to meet a Megalosaurus, forty feet long or so, waddling like an elephantine lizard up Holborn Hill. Smoke lowering down from chimney-pots, making a soft black drizzle, with flakes of soot in it as big as full-grown snowflakes—gone into mourning, one might imagine, for the death of the sun. Dogs, undistinguishable in mire. Horses, scarcely better, splashed to their very blinkers. Foot passengers, jostling one another's umbrella in a general infection of ill temper, and losing their foot-hold at street-corners, where tens of thousands of other foot passengers have been slipping and sliding since the day broke (if this day ever broke), adding new deposits to the crust upon crust of mud, sticking at those points tenaciously to the pavement, and accumulating at compound interest.

In keeping with the book's title, the first impression this passage makes is depressingly bleak. How does Dickens achieve this? The paragraph consists of eight sentences. The first is mere elliptical place-setting: *London*. The second sentence defines the time frame and informs us that the Lord Chancellor is presiding at court. (Three paragraphs further on, the gloomy setting is equated with the Lord Chancellor's courtroom, but we do not know that yet). The paragraph's predominant mood is established in the third sentence, *Implacable November weather*. Partly, this is accomplished denotatively: November weather in London is not likely to be pleasant, and this particular spell is "implacable," that is, pitiless, relentless. But the sentence is also effective because of the sequence and combination of its vowels and consonants, as a good readers theatre actor will know upon "tasting" these three words.

Sonority and sense extend Dickens's purpose in the fourth sentence. Its ponderous nature depends as much on the aural qualities of "mud," "waddling" and "elephantine" as it depends on the mental picture it conjures. This sentence is demanding to interpret. To communicate it effectively, it must be spoken clearly without rushing, with minimal pauses taken at the commas. The actor might wish to highlight the commas with the musical symbol for an eighth-note rest. In the latter part of the sentence, the audience might have difficulty following the image of the waddling

Megalosaurus because of the interruptive phrase, *forty feet long or so*. An experienced actor will establish a tonal link between the words "Megalosaurus" and "waddling." The intervening phrase, *forty feet long or so*, might be marked with up- or down-slanted arrows to indicate it either must be pitched lower or higher than "Megalosaurus" and "waddling." (I might direct an actor unfamiliar with this technique to "hang your voice on a hook at 'Megalosaurus,' come down (or up) from there, then return to the hook when you reach 'waddling.'")

All these techniques apply to the fifth sentence as well. Its final section separated by a dash suggests a longer pause after *full-grown snowflakes*. The sixth and seventh sentences need to be spoken as if separated by a semicolon, rather than a period.

Dickens's eighth sentence is an object lesson in the necessity of careful textual analysis. Its beginning, "Foot passengers," is a trap that might trip up even the most experienced oral interpreter. A performer interpreting it "cold" might reasonably assume that "Foot passengers" is a subject whose verb will appear at some later point after the phrase that begins with "jostling." This performer might then erroneously decide to pitch the end of "Foot passengers" on an upward inflection (a vocal "hook") to be echoed when its alleged related verb appears. But this never happens. The eighth sentence is elliptical. Its first two words should be read aloud as if they were followed by a colon . . . *Foot passengers*:

An elliptical sentence is a kind of narrative shorthand that omits part of its thought. The reader is presumed to be sufficiently sophisticated to supply what is missing. In the eighth sentence, what Dickens left out might be rendered as "All day, foot passengers have been *jostling* one another . . . and *losing* their foot-hold . . . and *slipping and sliding* . . . and *adding* new mud . . . ."An experienced interpreter will stress the underscored verbs; they are the chief auditory guideposts for clearly communicating this complicated sequence to the audience.

The eighth sentence also contains another trap. The two verbs, "sticking" and "accumulating," do not refer to "Foot passengers," but to the "new deposits . . . of mud." Thus, the idea that begins with "sticking" is distinct and separate, virtually a ninth sentence. Since neither the syntax nor the punctuation permits a full stop, the performer must select some inflectional, dynamic and/or rhythmic device to delineate this new thought.

New problems of interpretation arise in the second paragraph of *Bleak House*:

Fog everywhere. Fog up the river, where it flows among green aits and meadows; fog down the river, where it rolls defiled among the tiers of shipping and the waterside pollutions of a great (and dirty) city. Fog on the Essex marshes, fog on the Kentish heights. Fog creeping into the cabooses of collier-brigs; fog lying out on the yards and hovering in the rigging of great ships; fog drooping on the gunwales of barges and small boats. Fog in the eyes and throats of ancient Greenwich pensioners, wheezing by the firesides of their wards; fog in the stem and bowl of the afternoon pipe of the wrathful skipper, down in his close cabin; fog cruelly pinching the toes and fingers of his shivering little 'prentice boy on deck. Chance people on the bridges peeping over the parapets into a nether sky of fog, with fog all round them, as if they were up in a balloon and hanging in the misty clouds.

The governing thought in the six sentences that comprise this paragraph is stated immediately: *Fog everywhere*. Sentences two through five are direct elaborations constructed in parallel fashion; only the sixth sentence introduces syntactical variety. This structural similarity is compounded by the repetition of the word "fog" and by other echoes and comparisons: ". . . up the river . . . down the river . . ."; ". . . the Essex marshes . . . the Kentish heights . . ."; ". . .great ships . . . small boats . . . ."

Sometimes, recurring words or phrases are delineated by speaking them on a series of rising and/or falling pitches, a device known as a *ladder* that may be traced back at least as far as the Elizabethan theatre.[5] Ladders may be marked in the script with ascending or descending circled numbers written above the recurring words.

A performer might be tempted to use a ladder as a method for repeating "fog" thirteen times without tranquilizing the audience, but Dickens surely intended "fog" to be as repetitive as a foghorn . . . and that is the interpretive clue needed for effectively performing this paragraph. Of course, good oral interpretation depends upon subtlety. The actor will not try to slavishly mimic a foghorn, but will merely hint at its morose sonority. One of the most important considerations of good interpretation is the auditory value of vowels . . . what emphasis they should receive, their pitch, their dynamic level, their duration. Note, for instance, the onomatopoeic possibilities of several words in this paragraph: *wheezing, cruelly pinching, shivering*. Though the foghorn tone of Dickens's thirteen "fogs" precludes significant changes in pitch, the performer still may vary them by adding or avoiding stress, by increasing or decreasing their volume and/or stretching or shrinking

---

5 A ladder passage in *Julius Caesar* (Act II, Scene One) contains a pun that demonstrates the very technique Shakespeare is using.

their duration. (This device can be shown in the script by drawing a horizontal line [macron] above a prolonged vowel or a bowl [breve] above a short one).

2. *The director's textual analysis*: In addition to the thematic evaluation discussed at the beginning of this section and the choice of an appropriate staging mode (see below), readers theatre directors assess scripts for several inherent or potential auditory values:

A CAPPELLA MUSIC—Unaccompanied singing is a legitimate employment of the human voice that may be effectively included in many readers theatre scripts. See, for example, Charles LaBorde's *Memorial*.

CHORAL SPEECH—Pyrotechnic vocal effects such as antiphonal speech, crossfading dynamics, multi-rhythmic declamation and/or unison passages may be particularly effective in illuminating the text—or these devices may self-consciously interfere with the flow of the performance. If used, they must be exhaustively rehearsed and balanced to make them integral and not just prima donna bravura.

We created such a moment in the second act of Jo Davidsmeyer's *Angel*. This is the sequence in the original script:

EXECUTIONER
Heil!

IRMA
And he had a dream that that greatness could be recaptured.

MENGELE
Heil!

(Montage: Hitler, crowds, swastikas, etc.)

IRMA *(raving fanatically now)*
No longer did we have to hang our heads in shame as our parents had done. No, I could shout to the world, proudly, Ich bin eine Deutscherin!

MENGELE & EXECUTIONER *(rising)*
Deutschland über alles.

MENGELE, EXECUTIONER & IRMA
Zieg, heil!

IRMA
Heil, Hitler! And when I heard him as a child, for the first time in my life I was proud of what I was, a German.

MENGELE & EXECUTIONER
Heil!

IRMA

And I knew then what our destiny was. We would rise to power once again, so that no one, ever, could force us to feel shame, make us feel as if we were beneath contempt, beneath the rest of mankind. We are not. We are a superior people.

MENGELE & EXECUTIONER

Heil!

IRMA

We are, indeed, the master race. And you will not keep us crushed beneath your heel. If there has to be a fourth Reich, and a fifth, and a sixth, whatever it takes, we will rise to the place we were destined to hold!

This scene offered a good opportunity for choral arrangement. With the author's permission, we devised unison and antiphonal effects involving five members of the cast, including two who were, by then, offstage. Here is the "Nazi rally" as The Open Book performed it:

EXECUTIONER

Zieg—

ALL 3

(EXECUTIONER, IRMA, MENGELE)

Heil!

MENGELE

Zieg—

ALL 3

Heil!

IRMA

Zieg—

ALL 3

Heil!

IRMA

And he had a dream that that greatness could be recaptured.

EXECUTIONER & MENGELE

Zieg heil!

IRMA

No longer did we have to hang our heads in shame as our parents had done. No, I could shout to the world, proudly, Ich bin eine Deutscherin!

ALL 3 *(singing)*

Deutschland, Deutschland über alles.

OLGA & DEFENSE ATTORNEY *(off stage, chanting)*

Zieg heil! *(ad lib, softly, to end of sequence)*

IRMA

Heil, Hitler! And when I heard him as a child, for the first time in my life I was proud of what I was, a German!

EXECUTIONER & MENGELE *(joining chant)*

Zieg heil! *(ad lib under)*

IRMA

And I knew then what our destiny was. We would rise to power once again, so that no one, ever, could force us to feel shame, make us feel as if we were beneath contempt, beneath the rest of mankind. We are not. We are a superior people.

ALL BUT PROSECUTOR (*a shout*)

ZIEG HEIL!

(Silence)

IRMA

We are, indeed, the—

ALL BUT PROSECUTOR

Master race!

IRMA

And you will not keep us crushed beneath your heel. If there has to be—

IRMA & EXECUTIONER

A fourth Reich and—

IRMA, EXECUTIONER & MENGELE

A fifth Reich and—

ALL BUT PROSECUTOR

A sixth Reich!

IRMA

Whatever it takes—

IRMA, EXECUTIONER & MENGELE

We will rise to the place we were destined to hold!

SOUND EFFECTS—The frank theatricality of readers theatre allows the actors to produce a wide range of sound effects: animal sounds, bells, the sigh of the wind, thunder. In addition to vocalizing, the readers may create effects by such simple mechanical methods as drumming on stools or the backs of their books, shuffling their feet, clapping their hands, and so on.

29

STAGING READERS THEATRE

Despite the modifications worked by its essential minimalism and presentationalism, staging readers theatre is basically the same as traditional theatre. Scenery, costumes and lighting may be reduced in scope and scripts, stools and music stands may or may not be in evidence, but the philosophy governing set arrangement and patterns of blocking is identical. Thus, when The Open Book staged Jo Davidsmeyer's *Angel*, the first act courtroom was positioned center stage with the title character's flashbacks occurring on a separately-lit raised platform at the end of the room. In the second act, most of the playing space was devoted to Irma's cell, with the Defense Attorney's cot placed on the raised platform. Blocking patterns between the two areas were no different from traditional theatre.

On the other hand, the two main actors in The Open Book's production of Caroline E. Wood's *The Immigrant Garden* were each mostly confined to a single playing area and hardly moved at all. This script was staged in a modified version of a technique derived from oral interpretation platform programs, a method that I personally call "strict oral interp." To understand its ensemble staging applications, it is first necessary to see how it works with a single performer.

In the purest incarnation of solo oral interpretation, the performer stands in one spot facing the audience, sometimes behind a lectern, more often just standing full front, book in hand. At the start of the program, the book is closed; its opening is like the raising of a theatre curtain. The performer introduces the literature he plans to share (personal proof), drops his gaze to the book, opens it, raises his eyes and establishes direct contact with the audience in his role as omniscient narrator. Then, and only then, does the performance begin. This procedure is analogous to the polarization process that occurs at the beginning of any well-directed play.

Let us assume that the oral interpreter is about to perform one of the most difficult selections in the late Emlyn Williams's *Readings from Dickens* (William Heinemann Ltd., 1954): "Mr. Bob Sawyer Gives a Bachelor Party," which is Williams's adaptation of Chapter 32 of *The Pickwick Papers*. In addition to an omniscient narrator, this demanding tour de force requires the actor to create ten distinct characters, two of them women: Ben Allen, Betsy the handmaid, Jack Hopkins, Bob Sawyer, Mr. Pickwick, Mr. and Mrs. Raddle, a nameless youth in "a shirt emblazoned with pink anchors," plus a child and his father in one of Jack Hopkins's medical anecdotes.

The clear delineation of this mob is partly a problem in vocal versatility; Williams himself employed eleven voices, including a landlady of awesome shrillness. But an experienced oral interpreter will also help the audience distinguish between these characters by "focusing" each along one of eleven different fixed sight lines.

This does not mean that the interpreter moves about the stage every time a new character speaks; remember, he is standing in one spot. Instead, when he has dialogue (and perhaps description) pertaining to a particular character, he consistently looks in one direction. Assuming that when he is the narrator he gazes directly at the audience, he can still maintain this full frontal position and yet introduce two more characters just by tilting his chin up or down. By focusing his eyes forty-five degrees to the left or right and inclining or not inclining his head, he can "place" at least six other characters—which brings the positional tally to nine.

This is one of the reasons why "Bob Sawyer Gives a Bachelor Party" is difficult to perform. Its eleven voices demand two more focal positions than are comfortably available. Once, while performing my own cutting of this episode, I kept the following chart handy to remind me which directions to look in while playing the characters:

	EXTREME LEFT	LEFT	CENTER	RIGHT	EXTREME RIGHT
Head Up:		Betsy	Mrs. Raddle	Pink	Anchors
Level:	Father	Sawyer	Narrator	Ben Allen	Child
Head Down:		Hopkins	Mr. Raddle	Pickwick	

Focusing characters along fixed sight lines is a valuable staging tool in readers theatre. For instance, it is a natural way to perform the podium speeches in Bernard Shaw's *Too True to Be Good*, a 1931 "political extrava-ganza" that is, de facto, one of the first true readers theatre scripts by a major playwright. We used a modified version of the technique in The Open Book's production of Jo Davidsmeyer's *Angel*. Partway through the first act, the Prosecutor and Defense Attorney talk to one another during a break in the trial. Their blocking in this scene, patterned on "strict oral interp," stationed them facing forward to the left and right of center. When addressing one another, each turned his head forty-five degrees left or right. At this angle, though the actors cannot see each other very well, the audience believes they can and, more important, sees both of their faces clearly. The position also easily permits the performers to deliver appropriate lines presentationally.

As mentioned earlier, the principal actors in our production of Caroline E. Wood's *The Immigrant Garden* were each confined to a single playing area and seldom moved from it. The positioning of Mrs. Beauchamp's writing table up left center permitted her the option of facing

31

the audience or turning her head one-quarter right, which enabled her to symbolically gaze in the direction of her foreign correspondent. Similarly, young Cecily sat at a small bureau and either focused forward or one-quarter to the left.

A row of flowerpots divided England and America.

MEMORIAL

Winner of the First Readers Theatre Competition cosponsored by The Fireside Theatre and The Open Book is Dr. Charles LaBorde, a Beaumont, Texas, native who holds theatre degrees from Lamar, Texas Tech and Ohio State University. A former college professor, high school drama teacher and principal, Dr. LaBorde has directed and designed more than fifty productions, has acted in Texas, Ohio and the Carolinas, and appeared on television in *Gore Vidal's Lincoln*. He resides in Charlotte, North Carolina, where he serves as Director of Visual and Performing Arts Magnet Schools for the Charlotte-Mecklenburg Schools. "A child of the sixties," he says, "my draft number was a lucky 76." Solidly readers theatre, *Memorial* was first produced in a shorter version played by high school students in 1983 on the first anniversary of the dedication. A production was later mounted at The Citadel in Charleston and was also performed in Belgium and France. The Open Book's New York production of *Memorial* opened March 9, 1995, at The Amsterdam Room with the following cast:

A COMMISSIONED OFFICER . . . . . . R. Mack Miller
THE DRILL INSTRUCTOR . . . . Jon Koons
THE SOLDIERS . . . . Jennifer Daniels
. . . . Laurence Kaiser
. . . . Jenny Lambert
. . . . I. Steven Liss
. . . . Wayne Markover
. . . . Kelli Melson
. . . . Penrod Parker

MEMORIAL

A Theatrical Oral History of Americans in Vietnam

by Charles LaBorde

AUTHOR'S NOTES:

CASTING AND EDITING

Memorial was written, in part, to answer a need I have always felt in searching for scripts for a company of actors—a need for a play that matched both the number and the sexes of my performers exactly. The script has no set number of roles, and the sexes of the characters are not particularly important. Obviously, most of the speakers are male, but even male roles can be assumed by females in this show. While I cannot envision an all-female version, a mix of males and females is desirable. A careful selection and assignment of roles can overcome any possible confusion in the minds of the least imaginative audience members as to the presence of females in combat situations.

The speeches in the play are identified by letters of the alphabet for the sake of convenience only. The same actor should not play "Speaker A" throughout the play. The lettering is used merely to indicate a change in speaker. The only characters who remain the same are the Singer at the beginning and at the end, the D. I., and the bitter soldier in the peace segment.

As a further aid in making the play adaptable to any group of players, many segments of the play contain more speeches than would be needed by a small company. Some speeches can be eliminated, based on the size of the ensemble. For example, the segment introducing the characters has almost two dozen speeches. The number of speeches should correspond to the size of the cast. It should be obvious to a competent director which speeches are essential to the show and cannot be cut.

As far as the question of cast size is concerned, the show can easily accommodate as many performers as necessary. In its original production, the cast consisted of ten males and six females. A subsequent production at The Citadel, in Charleston, South Carolina, had an eleven-member all-male cast.

Another problem for some producing groups may be the language of the show. Much of it can be excised and the show thereby cleaned up considerably. However, too much bowdlerizing will make the language anemic and unrealistic.

The author asks that any such changes necessitated by adaptations for cast size or for the sake of audience sensitivity be submitted to him for approval prior to production.

A NOTE ON THE USE OF MUSIC

The use of songs is strongly suggested as a means of evoking part of the spirit of the times of the late sixties and the early seventies. Throughout the text suggestions are made as to where to include music. Possible titles are also given. Please note: these songs are merely suggestions, and other songs may be substituted for those mentioned. In either case, permission should be secured from the songs's copyright holders before any public performance.

Ideally, all songs should be sung *a cappella.* When absolutely necessary, a simple piano or harmonica solo can add much to the mood. You should, at all costs, avoid too much instrumentation. My great fear is that these "numbers" would transform the show into a musical, which most definitely it is not.

A NOTE ON SOURCE MATERIAL

The play is based primarily upon interviews I conducted during the spring and summer of 1983 with six veterans of the war in Vietnam. All segments of the play recounting events in that country were taken from these men's stories. To flesh out their reflections on the homefront, the peace movement, and the dedication of the Vietnam Veterans Memorial, I relied on newsreel footage, textual accounts, and documentary films about the dedication of the monument. Such sources were often altered during the development process of the script. Many speeches were improvised by student actors after viewing newsreel and documentary footage about the war and the dedication of the monument. I then took those improvisations, committed them to paper, and further altered them for dramatic purposes. Nevertheless, the speeches developed in this way still bear a strong resemblance to words captured on film by newsmen and documentary filmmakers. They have the ring of truth. The words of the six men interviewed personally by me appear with no interpolations or additions. Likewise, the speeches in the final segment are taken verbatim from speeches and prayers offered at the dedication of the memorial. None of the descriptions, accounts, or stories in the play were invented by me for dramatic purposes. To the best of my knowledge, everything that follows actually happened to these and hundreds of thousands of other American men and women during our country's time in Vietnam.

THE PLAY

As the audience enters, a scrim is down as a front curtain. House lights make it mostly opaque, but if we can see some ghost-like movement through it as the actors make last-minute preparations, that is okay. As the play begins, the house fades and we are left in the dark longer than usual. Then faintly (is it really there?), we hear a reverberating sound. The pulsing gets louder. It is now recognizable as a helicopter rotor. Possibly some shots or explosions are intermingled. None of the sounds are real, but merely computer-generated, synthesized sounds. The noise becomes overpowering, as if the helicopter hovers in the auditorium, then it quickly fades, as if the person hearing it has awakened from a nightmare. Silence. The lights slowly burn through the scrim. The stage is lit with a blue wash of light. Dim area lighting picks out the actors lying in two neat rows like bodies ready to be shipped home for burial. A low-lying fog may enshroud the stage, but it is not essential. The actor down center slowly rises, and the scrim starts out. The fog, if present, pours off the stage and rolls into the house. It is cold and dank, reminiscent of the grave. The lights come up on a cyclorama that hangs at the rear of the stage. They are bright. The color is blue. The area lighting fades so that the lone figure is silhouetted, as are the surrounding "bodies."

The Singer begins to sing a song evocative of Vietnam, such as Billy Joel's "Goodnight, Saigon." As the song continues, the bodies begin to rise, one at a time, randomly, until they form two staggered rows across the stage. They are immobile once they rise. At the conclusion of the song, the Singer speaks for the first time.

SINGER

In honor of the men and women of the armed forces of the United States who served in the Vietnam War. The names of those who gave their lives and of those who remain missing are inscribed in the order they were taken from us. Our nation honors the courage, sacrifice, and devotion to duty and country of its Vietnam veterans. This memorial was built with private contributions from the American people. November 11, 1982.

(Note: The above speech is an inscription that now accompanies the Vietnam Veterans Memorial. Alternatively, the Singer may merely recite these words and not perform any song. As the speech ends, the cyc fades so that we are in darkness momentarily. The area lights then pop up. The actors are still in line, but they have

37

their hands at their sides, and we see their faces for the first time. They are young. Incredibly young. Almost too young to die. The area lights fade again, and the actors are in darkness. The actor down right is the only thing illuminated on stage. He speaks.)

NARRATOR

On Veterans Day in 1982, several thousand Vietnam era veterans gathered in Washington with their friends, their families, and their memories of the dead. Their purpose was to dedicate the Vietnam Veterans Memorial—a monument erected not to the imagined glories of war but to the all-too-real costs of it. Since for almost a decade no one else had seen fit to welcome these survivors home nor to build any monuments for them, they raised the money themselves to honor their comrades who had paid with their lives in Southeast Asia. They then organized this celebration—a homecoming for heroes who never got one. Because it was so long in coming, it took on epic proportions. There were five days of vigils and reunions. The survivors alternately laughed and cried. They partied to forget and, nevertheless, remembered. The climax of the week took place at the long, low, V-shaped black-granite memorial that was chiseled with the names of those who had returned from the war. A war none of us ever understood, none of us ever supported, and all of us came to blame on those who did their duty by going to fight it.

There were 57,939 names etched in that stone the day it was dedicated. Since then many more have been added, as has a statue of three soldiers gazing toward the names of America's sons and daughters lost in Vietnam. The names were chiseled in chronological order of the dates when they died. The first name was that of Dale R. Buis, an Army major who died on July 8, 1959. His hometown was Pender, Nebraska. The last name was Richard Vande Geer, Air Force second lieutenant. Died May 15, 1975. His hometown—Columbus, Ohio.

On Saturday, the day of dedication, it was windy and overcast. Rain threatened. It was cold. The ground in front of the wall was wet, and the feet of the visitors soon changed it to mud. And then the ballet began, a sometimes graceful, sometimes frenzied, ballet of hands—searching the black wall—searching for the names of the dead.

THE BALLET OF HANDS AND THE LITANY OF NAMES

(The cyc comes up and the actors are silhouetted or backlit. Slowly the actors's hands rise in a slow-motion dance as they search the unseen monument for the names of the dead—a buddy, a loved one. [The monument lies along the "fourth wall" and is in the shape of a

38

widely-splayed "V" with its point downstage center.] Down left, a woman who is searching begins to say the names aloud, as if searching for one particular name. Her voice is a litany that interweaves with the other speeches. Eventually, her voice does not fade between speeches, but becomes, instead, an undercurrent said with the other voices, the names rolling inexorably from her tongue. Finally, she finds the name she is seeking. She then tells her story, too, and the litany stops.)

WOMAN

Kyle Smiddy
Aaron B. Spalding
Dale C. Allen
Lawrence E. Bach
James A. Blakely
Lawrence J. Bolger
Francisco A. Mazariegos
Victor L. Burns
Franklin D. Byum
Jimmy E. Carter
James E. Crawford
Allan J. Damian

(The light, which first focused on the woman, now shifts to other speakers on their lines.)

SPEAKER A

Vietnam only lasted one year for most of us. But then you came home and you kept quiet. I been ashamed for fifteen years. Everybody said they didn't want to hear about it. They said it was wrong what we did. But today my shame is gone. I can't look at that monument and be ashamed of myself. If anybody looks up there and is ashamed, then it's all in themselves. God bless all those Americans up there on the wall.

SPEAKER B

That's my boy. He flew a helicopter. He'd earned a Bronze Star, a Silver Star, and the Distinguished Flying Cross. He was coming home in a couple of weeks. We're just glad to see this day has come. We love this wall. It has a lot of meaning for all of us. He died November 20, 1967. In Gang Ni City.

WOMAN

Jeffrey J. David
Anthony Dicesare, Jr.
Carl D. Dudley, Jr.
Lewis B. Gaiser
John P. Gannon

SPEAKER C

I thought I'd hate the damn thing, but I see all these guys' names on it, and I can't hate it. I love it.

SPEAKER D

The boat I was in hit a mine and broke apart. There was a half dozen of us on there, but only me and this second class gunny made it off. I was in bad shape, and he dragged me to shore. I never got a chance to thank him, because he bought it four days later. Four days later. He's on the wall, and I'm here now to thank him.

SPEAKER E

I got kinda mixed feelings. Only reason I come was to see if these three names are on it. That's all.

SPEAKER F

My boy's name is on it, and I'm proud of him and I'm proud of the wall.

WOMAN

Alejandro R. Godinez
Donald P. Hamilton
Allan R. Hoffman
Curtis D. Jackson
Freddie Lee Johnson

SPEAKER G

It's good to be one of the walking. It's good to be back.

SPEAKER H

This country sucks. How many years went by before we get recognized. This memorial is to the dead ones. Hell, they're the lucky ones. It's all over for them. But me, I get up every day and force myself to forget. Every day it hurts. Where's my goddamn monument?

SPEAKER I

I'm proud. Proud to be an American. Proud I fought in Nam. And all these other guys here today feel the same. We were all brothers. I got to know these two guys from up north somewhere. These guys grew up together. They were buddies, you know—went to high school together, joined the Corps together, and died together over there. One of them died in my arms. *(Pause.)* Excuse me, I got a lot of old friends up there on the wall.

SPEAKER J

I came here to pay my respects to the guys who ain't here anymore and to anyone who served. You know, the wounds still haven't healed. But I came to honor all these guys—the living ones around me and the dead up there on the wall.

(The Woman continues with the litany, while other speeches now continue simultaneously with her speech.)

40

WOMAN

Paul E. Kincaid
Clyde E. Long, Jr.
Charles A. Lynch
Frederick J. Brenke
Kenneth A. Millard
Dennis A. O'Connor
Michael Parker
Paul M. Rodriguez, Jr.
Jackie L. Sanders
James M. Shepard, Jr.
James R. Snyder
Edmund B. Travis
Rick J. Stewart
James S. Stassi
Richard L. Walker
Robert M. Waller
Stephen G. Wassenich

SPEAKER K

We lost 57,000 of our brothers. If you weren't there, don't spoil our celebration. Right or wrong, I'm proud I was there.

SPEAKER L

My son got killed trying to help some others. We got this letter that says there's lots of guys alive because of what he did. It makes you feel, that maybe it wasn't all in vain. He was there, but he never carried a gun. He was in the medical corps. He just had his little medical kit and his courage. You know what he wrote on the side of his helmet? "Praise the Lord."

SPEAKER M

There are sixty names of boys from my hometown, Gastonia, North Carolina, up on that monument.

SPEAKER N

I'm a Vietnam veteran, and I remember a lot of the guys I took care of in the hospital, but I can't remember any of the names. It never seemed to matter until today. But now it hurts to stand here and see name after name after name after name and realize that some of those are guys I treated. I watched a lot of them die, but I don't know which names are which.

WOMAN

Jonathan—(*At this point, the Woman finds the name she has been seeking. She stops half-way through the name.*) Far as I know, he only lied to me once—in his last letter. He said, "Don't worry, Mom. All I ever do is guard this bridge." And less than a week later, he was dead. He was on a mission, but he lied so I wouldn't worry. But he was a good son. He went off with two friends—all of them 19 years old. I found their names first, and now I found his — all on the same panel. It's funny. All three went away from our small town, all three went to Vietnam together, all three died together. Odds are at least one of 'em should have come home. It's a shame. You know, I pray every night. I pray for my boy's soul and for his two friends. And I pray we won't have no more wars. I got a grandson 17 years old. If I had to see his name up on another wall . . . My grandson is gonna join the Marines. He can't find a job back home.

SPEAKER O

God, it was a long year, the longest of my life. I was in the infantry, a line outfit. I got shot. My blood soaked into the soil of that goddamn country. Me and my buddy over there—he lost an arm and a leg—we love this monument. We found names of other buddies we lived with over there till they died. What good is a statue, anyways? It just sets there collecting pigeon shit in a park. But this wall means something. There are names up there. There are names of people I know. Every name was a life, a story, a memory to those of us who survived.

THE SOLDIERS INTRODUCE THEMSELVES

(Suddenly someone shouts "Attention!" and all snap to in one long row across the stage. Then a "Rest" command and all stand, arms clasped behind them. One by one, they step forward and introduce themselves. When finished, they do an "About face" and return to line as the next speaker steps forward. All should be very sharp. Very military. Very proud. These are soldiers now, not the civilians of the previous segment.)

SPEAKER A

I have been wearing the uniform of the United States Army for 27 years. Born and raised on the island of Hawaii until I was 18 years old, graduated from high school, decided to see the world, and I joined the Army. And I've seen the world. Oh, and I spent some of that 27 years in Vietnam.

SPEAKER B

When called up, I was working as a carpenter. My dad told me he was gonna try to get me out of it, but I said, "You do that and I'll never come home again. I'm going." I look back and I don't regret it or what happened. Well, of course, at first I wanted to die, but now I know I'd do it all over again if I had to. Okay, so I lost an arm and a leg, but I'm a better person today than before I went.

SPEAKER C

I started off as a private, worked my way up, of course. I'm an infantry officer. We were the guys whose mission was to close with, capture, kill, destroy the enemy.

SPEAKER D

I signed up right out of high school. Everybody I knew was going right into college, but I didn't see any reason to. I wanted to do something exciting, so I decided I'd go into the Navy. I started to go into the Army, but somehow I ended up in the Navy. I didn't think about there really being a war on. I mean, I saw it on the news at night, but that doesn't seem real, you know. My parents thought I was doing the right thing. They figured it was the best way for me to learn something, since I didn't want to go to college.

SPEAKER E

I was infantry, basically a pathfinder. I spent my year out in the bush. Every third day you got mail, every third day they brought in more food for you. Hopefully, it was more food and not ammunition. Basically that's what it was like.

SPEAKER F

I'm a qualified parachutist. I'm a qualified Ranger, a highly skilled professional at working behind enemy lines. I'm a highly skilled man in demolitions, highly skilled in killing people. I speak Vietnamese. I speak German. And I speak Japanese and some Korean. All of these skills were learned in the military.

SPEAKER G

I was a platoon sergeant, platoon leader, section leader, while I was over there. I was wounded six times. In '68, '69, and '70.

SPEAKER H

Second Marine Division, Bravo Company, Third Battalion, Fourth Regiment. My soul is bush. I am a grunt. Reporting for duty, sir. Ready to serve my time in hell.

SPEAKER I

I'm a blanket-ass Indian. A reservation Indian born on Birchwood Reservation, Wisconsin. My main tribe is Chippewa. I was a mean little son of a bitch, but I got a four year scholarship to the University of Notre Dame. I was a Mr. Cool, Mr. Know It All. Man, you couldn't tell this blanket-ass nothing. Went down to South Bend at 15 and got me a little hometown drunk to buy me a six-pack of beer. Walked back up to the dormitory, put it on the window, turned on my radio, threw my feet up. Knock at the door. Father Superior came in. He says, "Son, you have fifteen minutes to vacate this school." If you think I was gonna go home and tell a Chippewa Indian grandmother that I was thrown out of Notre Dame, who damn near had to go to the Pope to get me the scholarship, no way. She'd have killed me. So the fastest way out in those days was go in the Army and hide. Which I did for the next 32 years.

SPEAKER J

I decided to join the Army after nursing school—for the experience. I wanted to learn a lot about nursing as quick as possible. When I signed up, they told me I could pick my assignment, you know, my tour of duty, and I thought, "I'll go to Hawaii or somewhere in the Pacific." I didn't really realize what was going on with the war. I thought I'd just go over there and help sick people get well. I could never have imagined what I really did see.

SPEAKER K

Well, it was coming time of the end of my senior year, and I didn't have anything planned. I didn't really want to go to college. So I just decided to join the Marines. They were supposed to be the best, and I wanted to be one of the best. I wasn't really thinking about the war getting any deeper and I thought it might just be fun to go over there. I wasn't thinking of killing people. I just thought it might be a lot of fun. My father thought it was a good idea—might straighten me out—make a man out of me. My mother didn't want me to go, but it wasn't really her decision, so I didn't care.

SPEAKER L

I was in the Army. I was drafted. All the guys were out there saying, you know, "They didn't get me." All of a sudden you go to the mailbox and there's your notice, you know. My mother carried on. She didn't want me to go, but there's not much you can do really. And my father never really gave a damn about anything I did, so why should he start then? So it really didn't matter. No matter how they felt, I still had to go. So I went.

SPEAKER M

I was a flyboy. "Freedom through vigilance"—that was our motto. All told I flew 64 missions—half of 'em in Southeast Asia. The thing you prized over all was your wings—a very proud moment when you got them. A real status symbol—only 10% of USAF flew. Without them you were little better than an infantryman or a Marine.

SPEAKER N

Everybody said they didn't draft teachers. Well, they did, because I was one of them. I put it off as long as I could, although I felt eventually I'd go in. And sure enough, in February of '69, I enlisted three days before I would have reported to be drafted.

SPEAKER O

It was more or less a voluntary thing for me. I wanted the combat pay. And, you know, it was a lark, but then, I'm a tourist at heart.

SPEAKER P

I didn't decide to go. I didn't want to go. Well, part of me wanted to go and part of me didn't. I could see the Romanticism of it, but I didn't want to kill people. But I was too damn lazy to get out of it.

SPEAKER Q

I flew 300 missions. Four tours. I liked it. There's an excitement you can never get anywhere else. I had an excess of a hundred missiles fired at me. None of 'em hit. But a couple went by so close you could almost read the "Made in the Soviet Union" label on the side.

SPEAKER R

I was excited. Something was going on. When I told the other guys where I was going, they looked at me kinda strange. I looked at it more or less as an adventure. No more dangerous than getting into a brawl with the British Navy in Hong Kong. We won that one. (*Pause*) When I got back, I was sick of it. It was pretty rough. Vietnam made me grow up.

SPEAKER S

I was raring to go. I was thoroughly ready to do, and I expected to be killed. That was my destiny. When I left to go, I knew I'd never be back. I even got my dress uniform ready so it'd look nice when they buried me in it. I wasn't supposed to survive.

SPEAKER T

My unit was active. We were—as the expression goes—in the shit. We were a hard unit. Every time the shit hit the fan, some general said, "Throw them in." And they did. I think they wrote off our whole battalion and said, "These fuckers are dead. Use 'em up. How many we got left? Good, we can use 'em here." That's what they did with us. Everyday. All over the DMZ.

SPEAKER U

I was in Vietnam about five weeks as an observer as the North Vietnamese took over, three years after the US military pullout. All we were there to do was see how long before the fall and to evacuate the embassy. The majority of the population didn't care anymore—it had been going on so long.

SPEAKER V

I was eager to go. I have probably got the best collection in the world of army comics. I saw every war movie. I'd spend $15 a month on my fantasies—being an American soldier. I was absolutely upset that the war would be over before I could get there. When the Marines went in in '65, I thought, "God, I missed it by a year." I knew it would all be wrapped up before I could get in. I was a wound-up killing machine. I was a naive, brainwashed kid. Seduced by Sergeant Rock comics and John Wayne. I'd blow your fucking head off, if given the chance. Killing meant nothing to me. You were meat. Dead meat if I was ordered to do it.

SPEAKER W

But first there was basic, boot camp, six weeks in hell.

BASIC TRAINING

> (*On "Hell" all snap to attention. Every other man takes one step back to form two staggered rows. The actor down right plays the drill instructor, who walks along, looking at the trash he has to work with. When he gets stage left, he turns.*)

D. I.

Sing to me, children. How's Uncle treating you? SING!

(The actors run in place and recite together.)

ALL

We like it here. We love it here. We've found another home.
We like it here. We love it here. A place to call our own.
We like it here. We love it here. *Bulllllll-shit!*

*(They all stop at attention, bracing, chins tucked in. All are fearful. The
D. I. strides down the line, stopping to speak to one unfortunate.)*

D. I.

So you like it here. Why's that? Do you like the food? The recreational
facilities? Or do you just like me? I'm speaking to you, son. Answer when
I speak to you.

UNFORTUNATE

Yes, sir.

D.I.

Do you like it here?

UNFORTUNATE

Yes, sir.

D. I.

Now, don't shit me, boy. Why? Do you like the food?

UNFORTUNATE

Yes, sir.

D. I.

You shithead, I said, don't bullshit me. The food here looks like day-old
dogshit and tastes like my asshole.

UNFORTUNATE *(smiling, relaxing)*

Right you are, sir.

D. I.

What are you smiling for, soldier? Are you laughing at me?

UNFORTUNATE

No, sir.

D. I.

Do you like me, son?

UNFORTUNATE

Yes, sir.

D. I.

You *like* me? Are you queer, boy? Is that why you like me, faggot?

UNFORTUNATE

No, sir.

D. I.

But you *do* like me?

UNFORTUNATE

No, sir. Yes, sir. I . . .

D. I.

You don't know what the . . .

(The D. I. rags the unfortunate in dumb show. As he does so, we hear the thoughts of some of the others.)

SPEAKER A

Bastard. I hated him. I'll hate him always. Cruel. I was from a place where people cared about you. Even if you didn't like someone, you were humane to them. And he was not humane.

SPEAKER B

It's hard as hell. Get you up first thing. Work your ass all day, give you a few hours sleep, and next thing you know, you're at it again. It was harder for me. The only thing I could think of the entire time I was there was how much I wanted to be back, just go back home. That's all I wanted, just to get back home. I shouldn't have been there. I didn't do anything for them to do that to me. The officers treated everyone like shit. But my main trouble was from the other guys—all the teasing cause I couldn't do what I had to do. I couldn't do it. I was never prepared for anything like that. I wasn't brought up to go out and fight. I wasn't brought up to go out at 5 a.m. in the morning, crawling around on the ground like some kind of wild animal. I mean, I never even played football when I was a kid. I just wasn't prepared for it. I went in there and they called me "Cherry Boy." They called me everything. I wasn't . . . I just couldn't do it, and I just had to learn. But I did it. I had to. But the stronger I got physically, the weaker I got mentally, because they were breaking me down. I just really don't see how I made it. To be truthful, I don't see how.

SPEAKER C

I suppose all of us were a little frightened. They didn't tell us a lot about what was going to happen. They tried to scare you a little bit in basic and what have you, but nobody really oriented us to what to expect. And so I was a little nervous. But I knew in my heart that I was gonna make it through. I just felt I would make it. I was a Christian, and I felt like the Lord was gonna protect me. I just felt that way, and yet, I wasn't living too much of a Christian life.

(In the middle of the speeches, the mute D. I. obviously orders the Unfortunate to give him "25." The boy falls down and immediately does pushups.)

SPEAKER D

I don't think there's any way you can be prepared emotionally for something

47

like war. There's no way in this world, because you don't realize what it's like until you see it. No matter what they do to you in basic. It's not like John Wayne movies.

SPEAKER E

It was all very tough. It was all, "Yes, sir. No, sir." Get up before the sun and go to bed after. It's really tiring. And don't backtalk anyone. They put you through living hell if you did. If they spit in your face, you couldn't even wipe it off. You had to stand there at attention. They did it to me a couple of times, and I never really knew why. But I sure as hell didn't ask. Most of the time I hated being there. Sometimes you get to where you feel you actually want to kill one of the sergeants. That's how tough it is. But basic didn't really prepare me for Nam. Nothing could prepare you for that.

(Suddenly the volume is back up on the D. I.)

D. I.

Get up, you worthless bastard. I ought to have you shot. You know, son, when you was born, the best part of you ran down your mama's leg.

(This elicits a laugh from somewhere in the ranks.)

D. I.

You pussies laughing at me again? I guess it's all the excess energy. Let's all work it off with a few two-mile "wind sprints." Right face. Sing, boys.

(They turn right, doubling into a column of twos, and high step off stage, chanting "We like it here" again as they exit. The D. I. faces upstage, standing directly center, and watches them go. When alone, he executes a perfect about face and then speaks of his time in Nam.)

D. I.

There's three things that I love. I'm a God-fearing man, and I love my country and my flag and my Mama and that's it. Nobody else. Rest of the people, I don't know, I hate them. I think you have to be God-fearing, and you have to love your country and your flag. And you gotta love your Mama, because without your Mama you wouldn't be here. And everybody else just falls into place. The only thing I don't like about my Mama is she's not parachutist qualified. She can't jump out of an airplane worth a shit. When you're in training, you're under constant pressure, constant harassment. Constant harassment and pressure, pressure, pressure. And the purpose of that is to make you function under hardships. If you're not capable of functioning under combat conditions or hardships, what the hell good are you gonna be in the field? So this is why, while you're learning to be a soldier, you're under constant pressure, constant harassment, constant hardship. To psychologically, as well as physically, prepare you, so that under combat conditions, when times are hard, times are bad, and people are shooting at you, that you're able to stay in control. If everybody just becomes a coward and sticks their head in the ground and hides there and doesn't shoot back, well the enemy's just gonna walk up on you and—*bang, bang, bang, bang*. After six weeks with me, you were ready for Nam. And it was you who was going to do all the fighting. This war was fought mostly by platoons—by enlisted men and a handful of junior officers. All the generals were back in their air-conditioned quarters in the rear. They got to sleep in real beds with soft sheets. They watched movies and ate food shipped in from Japan. Occasionally, they flew out to the war to see how things were going. But they were always sure to be back at HQ in time for lunch. Us guys in the bush never really knew what the goal of the war was. All we knew about was the objective of the day, which was usually some worthless piece of shit terrain that we would bleed for during the day and then abandon that night. There were no dramatic missions. Nothing to feel a part of. When your year was up, you just went home and the war went on with some new grunt counting backwards from 365. It made no sense to me or anyone else. Given that situation, I understood my platoon's true mission. No matter what the colonels and the generals told us, the mission remained the same. Our mission was to survive.

ARRIVAL IN VIETNAM

(As he finishes, the cyc changes color and actors reenter one at a time, as they describe arriving in Vietnam. They stand randomly about the stage.)

SPEAKER F

We got on a Flying Tigers Airways—never heard of it in my life. After a long, grueling flight, we're flying into Cam Ranh Bay, and I'm thinking, "Well, are they gonna issue weapons on the plane or what?" We used to say our butthole's getting tight. That's the way it was then. So we landed all lit up in the middle of the night. First thing you hear is artillery going off. *Boom, boom, boom, boom, boom.* You think, "Oh, my God, they're attacking the harbor, and I don't have a weapon." And all these *lights*, you know. That is what you go through. So you get off the plane and lights everywhere, the runway, you know, all lit up. You run for cover. Nobody told us what was gonna happen. Are they gonna issue me something to defend myself with? Are they really overrunning the base? What is it? You find out later that the artillery goes off constantly. After a while you just get used to it.

SPEAKER G

First night in Dang Ha, we were in hardback hooches, they call them—like summer camp houses where you have the cots and the screen windows and the roof. We were in those and the siren went off, and Dang Ha was getting shelled. So naturally from training, I went running outside looking for the first bunker I could find. So green I didn't think to look for one before the sun went down. And I didn't know the place. So I went running for what looked like this huge shelter and ran inside. Tunnels, and it was *hard*. Yeah, I got down, and the shells were going off outside. I could hear 'em and hear the siren going off, and I was safe. I remember thinking, "How come no one else is in here?" Anyway, I decided it was the safest place in the world —a super solid bunker—and I wasn't about to leave. Next morning I woke up and saw I was in the ammo dump. My first night. Thank God they didn't hit that place. They never would have found out where I went. "Gee, I wonder what happened to that new guy. Never saw him again." Vaporized.

SPEAKER H

The first night I was there, I went to my bunker. Night fell. I was the only one in there. I had on my boots. I put on my flak jacket, my steel pot, and got my weapon, and I laid on my back. And I thought this was the stupidest, the dumbest thing. But I laid there like that all night.

SPEAKER I

When I first flew over Nam, we were over the central highlands. We were headed out to the Gulf, when we developed a little emergency. I'm sitting there and all of a sudden this smoke starts floating past my eyes. I said, "Oh, dear." I turned around and the plane was full of smoke. You couldn't see a thing. Then I happened to look out the window and got another thrill. The propellers on two engines were just *stopped*. So we dumped our fuel and headed back to Da Nang. When I got off the plane, I was in a half crouch. I just knew a rocket was gonna get me. Shrapnel was just covering the runway, which showed you how many shells they received there. After I got my courage up, I just went around and picked souvenirs of the stuff up off the ground. That was my introduction to Vietnam.

SPEAKER J

I had a very interesting first night I was in Vietnam. They issued us a canteen belt and a canteen. Lot of good that's gonna do. Later on, I'm sitting around on my bunk, writing letters, wondering what's going on. And this guy runs through the barracks just in a panic. Wants somebody with O-positive blood. Somebody had set off a Claymore mine and blew himself almost to pieces. There I am writing letters, scared to death, and here's this maniac running up and down the building screaming for blood. Welcome to Vietnam.

SPEAKER K

They sent us out to our first line company. And I remember walking over this dike into a rice paddy and you know, "God, where the hell am I? Must be Vietnam." And all of a sudden, muddy looking creatures rise out of the ground with rifles. "Yeah, here comes the replacement." That was it. They handed me a rifle and very next morning we went out on my first mine sweep action. I had a dirty rifle, nothing to clean it with, and somebody gave me a few rounds of ammo. Didn't even have a magazine. So I had to crawl back to a place where I knew some CB's were, and I swiped a couple of magazines from them.

SPEAKER L

We took sniper fire on my first patrol, and I slammed down into the mud. And I remember the old guys all saying "Where's the new guy? How is he?" The new guy was laying face down in the mud. Furious. I was ready to kill. This was my moment. This son of a bitch had fired at us and made me get down and get wet. And I was miserable. And I was uncomfortable. The "new guy" was fixing his bayonet and starting to crawl forward. I was furious. I mean, no fear, nothing. I was ready to get out there and beat that sucker's ass.

SPEAKER M

There's two kinds of people in Vietnam: there's grunts and there's those who are not grunts. Those in the field—in a line unit—and those who are not. And, of course, when we arrived in Nam our biggest horror was to be put with a line unit, because we knew already that would be the worst deal we could get. And, sure enough, it was.

(The last actor to enter introduces us to the patrol segment.)

SPEAKER N

Everything operated from what was called a base camp. And everything was secured within this area. We had houses there, we had places to sleep. The unit I was in, the 25th Infantry Division, their base camp was in a place called Ku Chi. Twenty-five miles north of Saigon. And at that area we had our headquarters, we had our hospital there, our communications. All our support elements was located there. The fighting forces was outside of our base camp, and we'd get on our helicopters, on our slicks, and we'd fly out and stay out four, five, six days, sometimes for a month or so.

D. I. *(calling out)*

Fall in. Time for today's fun and frolic in the sun. S and D on the DMZ. Son, you take point. Okay, move out.

ON PATROL

(We are now on patrol. We hear for the first time about the line soldier in Vietnam—the life in the bush. As usual, the actors speak directly to the audience. As they fall in, the actors form a single line, but it is staggered such that we can see two men at once. After each speaks, he peels off right or left and goes to the rear in a sort of double endless loop. (The cyc is up green, and a single light illuminates the down stage part of the column.)

SPEAKER A

That's the way the war went. It was just a lot of patrol, shoot, never see anything. Just always out there. Never knew what the hell you were doing. Couldn't figure it out.

(From somewhere in the line we hear the following:)

SPEAKER B

Where are we going today?

SPEAKER C

Who knows?

SPEAKER D

We're on patrol.

SPEAKER A

We were a small part of a grand thing happening out there, but the individual soldier doesn't know jack-diddly about what's going on. The average soldier doesn't know shit. That's what Vietnam was like. You didn't know where the hell you were. You just knew you were on a stupid patrol somewhere in the boonies.

SPEAKER E

We were moving down the road and rocket fire starts coming on the road, so our brainy commander decides—I don't know what the fuck he decided—we're gonna outrun the goddam things or something? But he starts:

(From somewhere in the line we hear "Double-time" and all the actors run in place.)

SPEAKER E

And this whole damn company of Marines is double-timing down this damn road. And rockets are landing everywhere on the road. Finally, he says:

(From somewhere in the line we hear "Fuck this. Pull out. Get down and get cover." The actors then all fall flat. They remain in their two-man front.)

SPEAKER E

So we got down on the ground off the road, and I damn near killed myself right then and there. I dove on a damn bamboo shoot. Caught that right in the gut. Oh, that felt great. So I was pissed already. The rockets came in, and they were walking 'em in on us. *Blam, blam, blam, blam.* About six and we hugged the dirt. *Blam, blam, blam, blam.* About six more. *Blam, blam, blam,* and I'm thinking, "God, that one was close. Next one's got us, baby . . . ." And it never came. They had us and they decided not to shoot any more, or they just ran out of rockets.

(The second soldier in front eases up, while all the others continue to hug the ground. He uses the previous speaker as the other person in his story.)

SPEAKER F

I'll tell you about the scaredest I ever been. This was during the monsoon season, when it pours rain all day. We were out on ambush patrol. And I had my people, we were sitting alongside of a trail, a road. And I was squatting like this and my radio operator was right next to me. We were right at the edge of the tree line, right next to where the trail was. And I got the signal from up there, "Somebody's coming down the trail." So I passed the word back up, "Let them come." Because if you're going to spring the ambush, you don't want to get just one guy, you want to wait until it's the mass of the enemy in that kill zone. And then you trigger it. So, just let them pass on by. And we started counting 1, 2, 3, 20, 30, 40, 50, 100. Oh, Lord almighty, here we are 20 of us, and here was a hundred, and they were still coming. And what it was, was the lead element of a regiment. About 750 men. And I said, "No way in hell. The odds just are not right." And then one guy in the enemy group got the urge to take a piss. And he stepped out of the trail, and I'm sitting here—it was raining and I guess he couldn't see us—I'm sitting here and my radio operator's there and this guy's pissing on my radio operator. Talk about a pucker factor. Only sound I heard was this "*Sssssss*" and that was my butthole sucking my drawers. Let me tell you. Because if he'd a seen us, we'd of been like Custer at the Last Stand. 750 against 20. Wouldn't stand a chance in hell. So he peed on my radio operator and he just sat there and didn't move at all.

D. I.

Okay, men. Let's move the hell out of here.

(All the actors rise and resume the patrol.)

SPEAKER G

There's two types of climate there, hot and hotter. There's the dry season and the wet season: monsoons. The country is hot during the day and cold at night. You have the jungles, War Zone C, and when I talk about jungles, I mean jungles that we needed a machete to cut through. And then the mountains, and the flatlands, and finally the delta, the richest part of the country, where all the rice grows. And for miles and miles all you see is rice paddies. And rice paddies got water in them. Water everywhere. So, it's flat and it's long and it's wet.

SPEAKER H

When it rained, it rained. You stayed wet. You stayed cold. You stayed dirty. I went 72 days without a bath, when we went into Cambodia. Oh, I took a bath every night: got my steel pot, got a little water, washed underneath my armpits, washed my face, always my face. Brushed my teeth. Gotta brush your teeth. If not, your teeth'll fall out. Gotta take care of your teeth. Once underneath my armpits, between my legs, and my toes. I was ready to go. That was a bath to a grunt, for a soldier, for an infantryman. You smell? Yeah. You don't care. Do you use underarm deodorant? No. Why? Smells good, it smells good. The enemy is just as stinking as you are. You put some underarm deodorant on you, and you go into the jungle. See if you can't be smelled.

SPEAKER I

Oh, the bugs. There were leeches all over. Especially in the swamps. When they got on you, they sucked on you, and you had to take a cigarette, *whoosh*, and he popped off. Oh, I got leech bites all over me. And mosquitoes. Snakes. They had a mean snake about that long known as the "two step." He bit you and you took two more steps, bye, you're gone. There were tigers and monkeys. Beaucoup monkeys. Means a lot. Monkeys are good eating. When I worked with the montagnards that was a delicacy—monkey. Monkey meat. They also made good squeak-squeak soup. Mouse. I guess it's okay. I'm still alive.

SPEAKER J

Usually you got around by using the Chevrolet. You "shev" one foot down and you "lay" the other one behind it. And you kept a goin'. You humped in the woods. Day after day.

SPEAKER K

Uncle Sam was good about one thing. He gave you everything you need. He gave you all the bullets you wanted. He gave you all the hand grenades you wanted. You didn't ask how many should I have, you said, "How many can I carry?" And you just loaded yourself. I think I carried 52 magazines on me in a big bag one time. I had about 120 pounds of junk on me most of the time in the field.

SPEAKER L

And we used all that shit. We run into a fire fight between a hilltop here and a hilltop over there, shooting back and forth. Nobody could see a damn thing. Everybody getting off a lot of what I call sound shots.

(From the line we hear: Over there, Over there, That way.)

SPEAKER L

Buddadduddadut. Typical U. S. servicemen in combat. Use that ammo, buddy. Our platoon was sent around this hilltop to try to envelop it. About that time two of our tanks came down the road, and they saw this force coming around behind and instantly thought, Ah, ha, they re getting behind *our* boys. And they shot like the rest of us. The 90 mm beehive opened up—about a thousand little darts—they looked like miniature rocket ships—and they just sliced into us. So they greased a shitload of our guys right then and there. I remember one guy, his dick had been split right in half—just like an overcooked hot dog. Just *(whistle)*. Both sides doing this number. Ah, shit.

SPEAKER M

My philosophy with ammunition was this: it's hot out there and this shit's heavy. I carried one bandoleer with seven magazines —that's 140 rounds. If I'm in any firefight where I need 140 bullets, by the time I fire that last magazine, one thing's gotta be true—whole lots of other guys aren't alive anymore. I'll take theirs. If I get killed, what the hell did I lug around four bandoleers of the crap for someone else for?

SPEAKER N

Gold Company was coming around the base of this hill and Echo Company was coming across the top. And all of a sudden, one shot rang out. *Pow.* And every motherfucker—sound shots.

(As firing breaks out, all actors run for cover at front of the stage.)

Up there. *Brrrrr.* Well, the fools up here say, Down there. *Brrrrr.* Whole damn firefight started between Echo Company and Golf Company. We killed a lot of Marines. We shot up a lot of our guys. Finally, people are screaming, Cease fire. Cease fire. Cease firing. We get sent up the hill. I remember, I jumped over a bush, and there was one of the enemy. A Marine. That's one of ours, some genius said. And this guy was just laid out all full of holes. He was dead. Wounded lying all over the place. And they were all Marines. Gold Company I don't think took one hit. Echo Company couldn't shoot worth a shit, I guess. We waxed about nine guys of Echo Company. Stupid mistake. Whoever fired that shot, I'd give him the North Vietnamese Fucking Medal of Honor. That little fucker. He probably was in a little spider hole in the side of the hill, stuck his head up, and went *pow* one time and disappeared. But that guy had balls, and he screwed up a whole damn company operation doing that.

(The group is scared now. The next speeches reflect their confusion and fear as they take cover. The cyc fades and a light plays only on the speaker.)

SPEAKER O

War is hell. War is hell 'cause you're constantly under physical and mental pressure. You're scared out of your gonads. From the time you arrive there until the time you leave. And any person that says he wasn't scared—something is wrong with him.

SPEAKER P

All them goddam John Wayne pictures. That old crap that portray what we went through. That's nothin'. You know, that's nothin'. You know, that's zero. That was zero.

SPEAKER Q

The life of an individual soldier was one of constant fear, because you were always, you know, "Am I next?" It's scary. And you make all kinds of promises.

SPEAKER R

Think you could kill someone? If you'd tell me, "Oh, I could never do it," I'd call you a goddam liar. Let someone put a bullet through your arm or shoulder. Then you realize, if I don't do it to him, he's gonna do it to me. Like General Patton said, "Let the other son of a bitch die for *his* country."

(Lights on the cyc come back up as the D. I. speaks.)

55

D. I.

Up and at 'em, men.

(All rise and resume the patrol. This time the line follows the curtain line, moving stage left to stage right. The patrol is silhouetted in mime walking. A single light picks out the speakers.)

SPEAKER S

There we were in a foreign country whose people had no idea of what democracy was, trying to sell them on democracy. Trying to stop Communism. Didn't know who the guerrilla was, because he was everywhere. He was everyone. Anything that moved at night was bait. If you had to go to the bathroom after 6 o'clock, you better squeeze hard, because if you were seen walking outdoors to the toilet or whatever, we saw you, you were dead. The only people that moved at night were the enemy. I don't care who they were, they were my enemy and I shot 'em.

SPEAKER T

Down in the delta area it was guys in black pajamas, Luke the Gook, Local Yokels, and things like that—we referred to them—they were called Victor Charlie or Viet Cong. When you got up more towards the central part of the country, they called him "Charlie," and he was a little bit more sophisticated—he was closer to North Vietnam—he was better trained usually, better equipped. Sometimes in khakis, sometimes in black pajamas. When you got up on the DMZ, you were fighting hard-core North Vietnamese Army, and we called him "Mr. Charles." So you had Victor Charlie, Charlie, Mr. Charles.

SPEAKER U

"Sir Charles" a lot of Americans called him, because he was a good fighter. And I never underestimated the enemy. We did not fight a sophisticated enemy. We fought a guy that used a crossbow. He took bamboo, made little stakes, little barbs on the side, stick in the ground, called pungi sticks. He'd take a little human feces, dip it in there, and when it goes inside you, whatta you got? Infection. Very simple. Nothing fancy. Nothing sophisticated. Take some berries, mix it up, a little poison, shoot you with that bow, hit you anywhere and that poison's gonna take effect, gonna kill you, slowly. He didn't have atomic bombs. He did not have fancy weapons. A dedicated, fearless soldier. And initially when we went in, we didn't know that. Or if we were told that, we didn't believe it.

SPEAKER V

The guerrilla was the girl who came—"Hey, GI, like boom-boom? Two dollars. Good time." While you were having a good time with her, her girlfriend was writing down all the troop positions. She was giving you VD, and you became a casualty, you had to go to the rear, you had to be evacuated. Or she just cut your throat.

56

SPEAKER W

Or the little kid. "Hey, GI, you want buy a Coke?" And inside the Coke bottle—little slivers of metal or even feces—he went to the bathroom, mix it up with water, put it in the Coke, gave it to you. Something sophisticated about that? "Hey, GI, you want ice?" I don't even want to think about what was in that.

SPEAKER X

In the field units we didn't have racial problems. You know, everybody was buddy-buddy. Nobody was a nigger or a dago or gook or whatever. When you got in that foxhole, you were buddy-buddies, and you didn't care whether he was black, white, red, green, purple, because your life depended on his and his life depended on you.

SPEAKER Y

We didn't have discipline problems in the bush, in the field, because we had to trust each other. And that's the biggest thing. Everybody did things right. And if somebody did something wrong, blew a little choke, we took care of 'em in our own little ways. We'd give 'em a blanket party. You know, when a guy's laying down getting ready to get some Z's. You take a blanket and you throw it over him and everybody whips his ass, and he doesn't know who did it. This way he can't say, "You did it and you did it." Everybody would get a little bit of him. He knows. He won't say a word the next morning.

SPEAKER Z

And he didn't go to sleep on you, either. People didn't go to sleep on me in my outfit. I'd blow their ear off. One night I did something that was worse than that. I took his rifle away from him. I gave him a hand grenade, and I took the pin away. And I put him out there a couple of hundred yards by himself at night and said, "You gonna be my early security. You gonna tell me if the enemy comes." "But I don't have a gun." "You don't need no gun. But if you throw that hand grenade, this tells me that the enemy is coming. And if I hear that hand grenade go off, I'm gonna shoot everything I got in that area." So this guy sat all by himself, this hand grenade in his hand. He didn't go to sleep, 'cause if he went to sleep—*boom*—blow himself away. If he threw it, we'd shoot him. He was shit out of luck if the VC really had shown up that night. We had no problem with him going to sleep on us again. Never went to sleep on us again. He stayed awake after that.

SPEAKER AA

Strange things flash through your mind when you're under fire. Last time I really got shot up bad, we were making a sweep. I had 98 men, all Vietnamese, a young Army captain that I was trying to show the ropes, and me. I showed him the ropes all right. Led us all into an "L" ambush. The enemy allowed us to walk right in and then he opened up. The first burst hit a rock here, and I bled pretty bad from a head wound. Then the guy really started after me. I dropped behind a rock about this big and in about three seconds, it was that big. I went to roll to another rock and, as I was rolling, he fired another burst and he blew my M-16 apart. He shot a Rolex watch up and shot my hand almost off. Well, he starts shooting at that next rock and then a couple of my people come up and start shooting at him, so he starts shooting at them. So I'm gonna get away from him. There's some big rocks back there. So I start crawling. That bugger sees my big rear end crawling, and he shoots me dead in the butt. And I do a somersault. I crawl behind this rock. I got blood coming out of the back of my head. Out of my ass. My hand is laying there. My M-16's blown apart and guess what the first thing came into my mind. "That motherfucker is trying to kill me." And he was. Because I was trying to kill him. In fact, I did.

SPEAKER BB

That's the way the war went. Little isolated stupid things that didn't mean anything. There's no front line. They'd melt away, and they'd get us next time. 'Cause we're gonna come right back again. We never *went* anywhere and stayed there. In your isolated little area, you were just playing silly games back and forth, back and forth. It was just so stupid. It would have been funny. Except guys were getting killed all around you. Buddies.

(As the speech ends, we hear:)

D. I.

Fall out. Chow time, courtesy of Uncle Sam. Bon appetit.

(He pronounces it "Ap-uh-tit.")

AT EASE

(The general lighting comes up now as the actors form two very tired groups stage right and stage left. As they eat and rest, they tell stories. The group on the right is quite serious, the left more light-hearted. The scene alternates between the two.)

STAGE LEFT

SPEAKER A

We had sometimes one or two hot meals a day. Or maybe just one. They'd fly out a meal and feed us in paper cups and paper plates and fly back home. Green eggs in the morning. Eggs turn green if you keep them in a hot container for a long time. But most of the time we ate from the cans—C-rations. But one thing we loved more than anything else: we'd fight like hell for ice cream. Very seldom did we get it. And when we got ice cream, we'd fight for it. One thing we'd always eat, because it was always so damn hot over there. Ice cream. I fell in love with ice cream. Everybody fought for ice cream. That was a luxury.

STAGE RIGHT

SPEAKER B

Your mind is so blown up the first time you kill someone, you're so psyched up, you really don't think about it. It's not like an act of going out here and committing a murder. Maybe it does bother you. It may just be an act of aggression at that time, but when you're out there in the woods, in the bush, and this guy's shooting at you, well . . . The first guy for me was on an ambush. We were sitting, waiting, and he came walking across my sights.

SPEAKER C

I never regretted killing anybody. And the reason why is simple: it was either him or me. That's why I don't regret it. I had a job to do, and it was either I die or he dies and I wasn't gonna die. Sometimes I'd wonder about it, but yet at that time, no. I can say that I know of seven people that I actually killed. I may have gotten many more, but the seven—I can actually account for seven of 'em that I know I blew away. I know I got 'em. I watched 'em go.

STAGE LEFT

SPEAKER D

Greatest little hooker joint in the world. I remember the first girl I met. I was sitting in a bar with a guy. Just went into town for the first time, and I feel this weight on my shoulder, and I turn around and it's a right leg and I just turned my head all the way. Thing liked to jump out and bite me. It's right there with the skirt pulled up, and she says, "You Marine?" Boy, I think I have arrived. I've died and gone to heaven. Welcome to Saigon.

SPEAKER E

Thai ladies were nice, too. Yeah, they were real nice.

SPEAKER F

You needed to be careful, though. I heard they'd put razor blades in their snatch. You get a little paranoid after hearing stories like that.

STAGE RIGHT

SPEAKER G

Why worry about killing those bastards? When the North Vietnamese or VC would capture a South Vietnamese soldier, the first thing they would do was cut off his gonads—they'd castrate him. So most men didn't want to be captured because —you know, that's—it hits really close to home.

SPEAKER H

And I can remember they'd take a generator that'd generate 75 or 100 volts of electricity, and they'd hot wire the prisoner's gonads. And he talked. Oh, yeah, he talked. A human being can only take so much. After awhile of that, you see 'em start talking like a mynah bird.

SPEAKER I

Our South Viet allies weren't no better. I can remember us getting prisoners, and we'd turn them over to the South for interrogation. And these guys showed no mercy. They'd take two of 'em up in a helicopter and start asking them questions and then get up to about 1200, 1300 feet and ask them again, and "Un, un, un." *Bang*. Kick one guy off, and the other guy, "*Blah, blah, blah.*" As soon as they got what they wanted out of him, *bang*. Kicked him off, too. No witnesses. Right?

STAGE LEFT

SPEAKER J

USO shows would have some girls and jokes and singing and dancing and that's about all. They had a movie just about every night. You know, I saw *M. A. S. H.* for the first time in Nam.

SPEAKER K

Hell, the USO loved to bring out Bob Hope. Fly us in to see him. But who gives a damn about Bob Hope? Big deal.

SPEAKER L

There's something desperately wrong with morale if someone isn't bitching all the time.

SPEAKER M

Raquel came to see us. Dance with a GI. Rub against him and he'd get all hot and bothered. All for nothing.

STAGE RIGHT

SPEAKER N

When I first went to Vietnam, they were having trouble forming the Vietnamese army, because up to that point it wasn't much of an army. So they had a mass recruiting program. If you were between the ages of 16 and death, you were inducted into the army automatically. And I was taken out to one of their basic training outfits to show how to instill discipline. American advisor, you know? They had a large problem with guys going AWOL, because they didn't want to fight in the army. Well, before I could make any suggestions, their officers solved the problem themselves. They had a large formation with about 100, 200, 300, 400 guys in it, and the commander would come out in the morning, and he'd walk down the line and grab a guy and walk out in front of everybody, pull out his pistol, and *bang*. Shoot him in the head. And then say, "Now, this is how we deal with discipline problems." No one went AWOL anymore.

STAGE LEFT

SPEAKER O

The colonel was concerned about rumors of drug use. I said, "Colonel, they ain't rumors." When word got out we were gonna have a shakedown, it would rain marijuana out the windows.

(Overhearing the man stage left, a soldier from the right group walks over and speaks.)

SPEAKER P

Let me tell you a story. Perimeter. Two men in a foxhole. At midnight they're gonna be relieved. These two other guys are crawling out to relieve them. They crawl up to the hole, and these two guys, who are supposed to be protecting the camp, are in there with a joint, poncho over them. Puff, puff. "Hey, man. Cool." One of the guys crawling out tosses one grenade. *Boom.* The death certificate says, "Killed by enemy action." "Sarge, we got out there, and I'll be goddamned if a grenade didn't go off in the hole." Think about it. A lot of people back home will say, "Oh, they were wrong dropping a grenade down in there." But what if Charlie came through where they were and killed me back in camp? Right? All I know is one thing: I won't ever have to crawl out to relieve those two sons-a-bitches again.

(Another actor from the right group crosses, and the stage lights are coming up. The actors are one group again.)

SPEAKER Q

No wonder they're raising hell about the war back home, when they hear shit like that.

SPEAKER P

Back home. Yeah. Burn the goddam colleges down. Love, peace and sunshine.

PROTEST ON THE HOME FRONT

(As he starts this, the others move upstage, place headbands, flowers, etc. on to indicate that they are civilians, flower children. The cyc turns to blue and the area lights fade, a single light remaining on the speaker. As he continues to talk, the others kneel, as at a sit-in protest. They begin to pound the floor in a drumlike rhythm as they chant. The group keeps up this mantra-like sound under the following speeches.)

ALL

Give peace a chance. *(etc.)*

SPEAKER P

You know, before enlisting, I was in college. I resented the peace establishment even then, and I never dreamed I'd ever be in Vietnam. When they struck the school, I didn't participate in it. I was there to get an education, not a deferment. One guy came and gave us a speech telling us to fight for peace. Was he listening to what he was saying? To me the war was a job. I

61

got satisfaction out of it, but I wasn't there to kill people. I don't think I would have gotten satisfaction out of that. I was fighting for my country. I always felt like the people at home—if they just knew what we were doing—all the protests would stop.

(The lights fade on the soldier as the chant swells and changes.)

ALL

Hell, no, we won't go. *(etc.)*

(After some time the chant subsides to just the pounding. The lights return to the soldier as a lone female figure leaves the group and moves toward him.)

SPEAKER P

And I really loved the great American patriots like Jane Fonda. We heard her broadcasts from Hanoi. She deserved to be shot. She was supporting the Communists and everything. She was talking treason, flat out treason.

(The woman speaks seductively in his ear. The beat continues.)

SPEAKER R

Tonight when you are alone, ask yourself what are you doing. Accept no ready answers fed to you by rote from basic training. I know that if you saw and if you knew the Vietnamese under peaceful conditions, you would hate the men who are sending you on bombing missions. Have you any idea what your bombs are doing when you pull the levers and push the buttons? Should you let Presidents, generals, and other liars define for you who your enemy is?

(When she finishes, another actor may move from the protest group and sing a brief passage from a song of the era, such as "The Ballad of Abraham, Martin and John" or "Blowin' in the Wind." The lights then return to the soldier. "Jane" and all but one of the actors move downstage and sit casually with their focus upstage on the single remaining protester.)

SPEAKER P

Yeah, I remember Woodstock. "Give me an 'F.'" I'd like to give some of those bastards an "F."

(The light now goes to the protester upstage, who is going to tell his Vietnam story. He finds it very amusing.)

SPEAKER T

I really fucked up the minds at my draft board. I got out of college in only three years. They couldn't figure out why someone would shorten a possible four-year deferment to only three. It flustered them so much that they classified me ineligible for the service. I guess they had enough nuts in the Army, and they didn't need another one.

(At this point the protester may sing a wild version of some protest song, such as "Vietnam Rag." If such a song is used, he should pull people up from the floor. Those standing should assist him in dancing during the chorus. As he gets caught up in the frenzy of the moment, he should attempt to involve the audience, even getting them to sing along. If this device is used, the words to the chorus or refrain should be written on portions of the anatomy of the protesters—arms, legs, chests. The protesters pull clothing off, down, up to reveal the words so that the audience can sing along. If the song contains the word "Vietnam" or "War," it should be written on someone's ass or, at least, the seat of his pants, thus allowing the protesters an opportunity to moon the audience. As an alternative to the use of a song, the protester gets the group to take up their chants once again. He gets one section to do "Give peace a chance." Another does "Hell, no, we won't go." Yet another section can chant "Ho, ho, Ho Chi Minh." This chaos of sound is accompanied with the pounding. When it becomes too loud to be bearable, the lead protester collapses and the sound stops. When either the song or the chant is all over, the actors drop their protester persona. The lights fade and the cyc returns to green. We are now firmly back in Vietnam, and the actors are again exhausted soldiers on patrol. The lone speaker, who has stood stoic, at attention, throughout the fury of sound, now offers his final explanation.)

SPEAKER P

You see, I can't listen to those people back home who say the war is unjust, that we should get the hell out. That would mean we were wrong to be there in the first place and that the guys who gave their lives saving mine died for nothing at all.

NIGHT IN THE BUSH

(He rejoins the group, which slowly moves to form a circle center stage. They squat, sit, lie. The effect should be one of people gathered around a campfire. The circle should be more open on its downstage arc. Some of the upstage actors may want to be standing. As the circle is forming, one actor speaks.)

SPEAKER U

Nighttime was the worst time in Nam. Night in the bush was absolutely terrifying, because you couldn't see anything and you knew Charlie was out there and you never knew when he might be coming.

(The cyc fades. The scene is lit only with concealed flashlights held by the actors. By the time the lighting change is complete, one actor is in mid-story, with the lights focused on him.)

SPEAKER V

One night 68 Americans got killed, 34 wounded, and only 14 of us came out in one piece. I lost a whole bunch of people that night. The whole world came in on us. And it was over a piece of ass. You see, some guy had been out without security, and he found this little girl—who just happened to be Viet Cong—and she was having a time servicing all the guys in artillery at $2 a throw. It was just like a bunch of dogs lined up and that's how they were—like animals. She didn't care. I've seen Vietnamese whores make $200 in 30 minutes . . . I caught 'em and I made 'em go to the commander, and he let her go. And she took the sappers in the same way that she went out. Sappers are guys that first thing they did, they got their choke. Heads all blown away and they got their heroin, and they got all blown away. And they stripped off all their clothes, and they tied demolition to their body. And they went out, minds all blown away, searching for trip wires through the foxholes. Anyway, she knew exactly where the wires were, where the booby traps were at, and she brought the sapper squads in, and they blew the whole place apart. They attacked us from everywhere. And it's hell when you're just shooting, 'cause you don't know who you're shooting at. And I lost a real good friend of mine there. This guy was from New York City, and he looked just like Frankie Avalon. He used to say, "When I get out, I'm gonna meet Frankie." And he didn't make it that night. He didn't make it.

SPEAKER W

One night after a long hard day, including a fire fight, we dug in and moved off this hill into a clearing and dug in a 360. And I was on watch. In that platoon we never slept the whole night through. You were either on 100% alert or 50% alert. Never on anything less—in our outfit anyway. So you knew for a fact you were never gonna sleep more than four hours in a row. That's hell. So I'm falling asleep in this foxhole we dug. I remember my head was just leaning forward, and "*Clink*"—the helmet's hitting the edge of the thing. So I was really getting tired. I could not stay awake. I thought, "Oh, God, I can't stay awake. I'm gonna fall asleep. I'm gonna get my throat cut. The lieutenant's gonna shoot me. Something." So I figured noise, that'll do it. That'll wake me up. I tried the canteen. Dumped water on my head. Everything. Nothing worked. Still clinking against the foxhole. So I took out a grenade. I figured if I fired my rifle everybody would want to know what I shot at. Figured if I threw a grenade, no one's gonna know what happened. So I take the grenade and I pull the pin. And somehow or another, instead of going forward—I don't know—I was tired or what—but I threw the damn thing sideways. And there's another hole over there with a Marine sitting in it. And I think, "Oh, Christ." All of a sudden—*wham*. Blew the sucker back on his ass, and he gets up screaming, "Incoming. Incoming." And I start screaming, "No, no, you fool, it's mine." Now he's really in a panic, and he starts screaming, "It's a mine. It's a mine." And it went all the way around the 360. So I'm listening to this shit. "Enemy to the front. Mine. Enemy to the front. Mine." So it's going all the way around. Sure enough, I heard it coming, and I hear the guy on the other side of me say, "Hey." "What?" "Enemy to the front." "Right." And the guy comes around with orders from the lieutenant. "100% alert. 100% alert. 100% alert. Movement out there. Activity. We don't know what. *Blah, blah, blah.*" And everybody was up all night. Now I knew there was no one out there, because I threw that son of a bitch. So with everyone else awake to protect me, I just slinked down in my hole, and I went to sleep for the whole night. It was the best night of sleep I'd had in I don't know how long. I never told a soul 'til I got out of that platoon, because if anybody knew I'd kept them up all night long, I may not have made it.

SPEAKER X

I know that's how my lieutenant got shot one night. We shot the shit out of him ourselves. Cut his legs off. He lost both of 'em. Machine gun. He was a fool. He was an absolute fool. He sent me on an LP one time, and he got pissed off, and I lost my rank on this one. He told me to take my fire team out to a listening post on top of Dang Ha Mountain. You're talking two miles, across a river, and up 8 or 900 feet. About three miles all the way. Well, Mr. Charles owned that friggin' hill. And everybody knew it. That's where the hell they'd been shooting from all day long. And this jerk tells me to take myself and three other guys up that damn hill that night. For a listening post. So we figure, "Screw this shit." That's the kind of fool he was. We went out that night and laid down by the river. Every half hour or so, we'd radio in. We told him we were up on top of the hill. He found out about it. I don't know how. Somebody shot the shit with somebody, and the story got out. He chewed me out good, and I was busted down to "point rifleman." Suicide. He was trying to kill me—that's exactly what he was doing. And every time I went out on point, nothing happened. Not a damn thing. Every time someone else went out on point, somebody got killed. Point man got shot. I got to be a good luck charm. I even flushed out an ambush once, walking down a dry riverbed. What kind of a fool leads a platoon down a dry riverbed with wall embankments on either side? I mean that's the kind of bastard this guy was. One night, the lieutenant had been out playing silly games again. He was outside the 360. So this clown comes walking up to my machine gun in the dark, and I challenged him. "Halt. Who goes there?" And he didn't answer. Obviously, he was trying to play some silly games—"I'm so cool. I'm the lieutenant. I'm going to sneak up and find my men fucking off again." He was that way. I knew exactly who it was. But the guy didn't answer the challenge, so I followed his orders. I turned loose. I opened up. He was laying out there screaming, "You son of a bitch, you son of a bitch, you son of a bitch." He just kept repeating that over and over again. The result was, he lost both legs. It couldn't have happened to a nicer guy. Jerk tried to get me killed. I know for a fact he got one of my friends killed. He sent an ambush to the same site five days in a row. And on the fifth day, Charlie was waiting for 'em.

To hell with him. I'm glad he did lose both his legs. That kind of thing can happen. You piss somebody off bad. What the hell.

SPEAKER Y

The worst thing I saw in Nam was at night when I was guarding the loading of a boat with civilians. A South Vietnamese cop was supervising the actual boarding, you know, making sure people only took one personal item on board with 'em. Then up comes this ugly South Vietnamese woman with a pig under one arm and a baby sucking on her right tit. The policeman stopped her, and I guess he explained the one item policy. It was dark, and I really couldn't see too good. Anyway, she stooped down near the water, and I heard a splash. She stood up, and I saw her shadowy figure get on board. A few seconds later from the boat I heard that pig squeal, and I knew what she had done. You see, she could always have another kid, but that was probably the only pig she'd ever own. (*Pause*) Goddam, I wish this was all over.

> (*There is an impossibly long pause after the final story. Then one actor begins to sing a mournful song, such as "Homeward Bound," and the others quickly join in. They stay in the circle, their lights the only illumination. The lights snap off one at a time at the conclusion of the song. The actors then break the circle and move one at a time to their random spots about the stage. When each actor reaches his spot, he snaps on his light, illuminating his face, and says his speech.*)

COMING HOME

SPEAKER A

It's a very, very long year. Of course, you count your days. You know how many days you got left. Course, you get down to 90 days or so, you're "short." Getting shorter and shorter. You get more careful, the shorter you get.

SPEAKER B

The universal fear was your last mission. Like you feel it's on your last mission you're gonna get it. Hell, you could be on 20 flights, and you wouldn't worry 'til number 20. Then you say—I've got one to go—this has got to be the one that gets me.

SPEAKER C

I'm trying to hitch a ride to get to base so I can fly home to the States. Finally I got one—with a fuel truck. Fifteen miles in the dark, riding back to base in a fuel truck. Talking about having a tight one.

SPEAKER D

And suddenly, it's over. When I got back on the plane home, I had this weird feeling in my chest. And I'm thinking in this plane going home, "Well, I made it twelve months in Nam. Now I'm gonna die of a heart attack right here in this plane."

SPEAKER E

Over there the maximum speed was about 35 MPH. So when we got back, we had a cab driver taking us from the base to San Francisco, and on the interstate he was doing 55 or 60. We were all sitting there hugging each other saying, "God, slow down." Here we were flying in jets over Nam for a year and a half, and now we're hiding on the floor of a cab rocketing along at 55. We thought we had been brought home only to die at the hands of a daredevil cabby.

SPEAKER F

You sense the antagonism as soon as you get back. No one was there to pat you on the back or say you did a good job. No one was there to say, "Hey, come in here and have a drink." You stood in line to catch the airplane like everybody else, and they tended to look at you funny, because you were wearing a green uniform.

SPEAKER G

I had some problems when I left the service. I remember standing around at the airport in San Francisco, and these hippies starting spitting at me. And then there was four college types, from Notre Dame I think, when I was at O'Hare, giving me a load of shit about how I should of gone to Canada instead of Vietnam. I remember all that shit, and I'm telling you, I'll never forget any of it.

SPEAKER H

When I came home, people called me "killer." I mean, people I *know*. And they'd see me and point. You know, "Here he comes now." I don't care how much you hated the war, you shouldn't spit on the warriors. I did my duty. Maybe I wasn't a hero, but I damn sure should have been allowed to come home with some honor.

SPEAKER I

I got spit on—by kids. Why? Because I was wearing my uniform. But even harder to take was my family. They were scared of me, even said I was crazy. But that's all history. I've gotten on with my life. But it's still hard when I think back, and it's hard to forget.

SPEAKER J

Everybody wanted to paint us as different. News headlines like, "Berserk Vet Kills Family of Five." But most of us tried to take the killer out of our souls and live the American dream again. That's what I've done, you know. I'm an American, and I'm a veteran of a war that nobody seemed to want me to win. Well, let me tell you, I'm proud to be both an American and a Vietnam vet.

SPEAKER K

I remember getting off the damn plane, being carried off the plane at LaGuardia Airport. Here we are wounded, getting off the plane, being carried on stretchers, and a bunch of shitheads out there with signs saying,

"Baby Killers." Shit like that, you know. By that time it really didn't matter. We didn't think much of 'em. It had turned us against them—our own countrymen, as if they were some sort of subhuman life form that was the enemy. And we were all American snuffies with puppet strings on us, playing the game whenever the big boys pulled the cord. And yet the whole country had been turned against each other. And so there they were—American kids, housewives, mothers— holding those signs. I hated them so much. Pack of worms. They were dead to me.

SPEAKER L

I remember the first time when I got home, I got in my car and drove out in the country, and I was just in a daze. 'Cause I was driving along the road, I was looking at the trees, and I was thinking, "You know, there's nobody out there wanting to shoot me." It was good to be home.

THE WALL AGAIN

(The lights change again. The flashlights all snap off, and the cyc comes up blue. The hands again do their ballet, as the actors move into a line across the front of the stage. We are clearly back at the memorial wall. The speaker is illuminated. When each finishes, he moves back to his original position at the beginning of the play. Once in place he stands rigid.)

SPEAKER M

Vietnam. It's with me all the time. I can't forget it. I just can't forget it.

SPEAKER N

I hope the war was worthwhile. But we should have really gone in and fought it. Now people are saying Vietnam wasn't worth it. I just don't know. It's hard to justify the deaths of lots of friends when I look back now and see how we just quit. Just walked away.

SPEAKER O

I got a belt at home with some blood on it. I took it off a guy threw a grenade at me. I mean I think I shot about 40 rounds in him. I got his little pistol, too. A Chinese 9 mm. He was an officer. Only officers carried pistols. Now, listen, I was not a—I mean, I didn't go around stealing things off bodies, okay? No, I wasn't one of those perverts. Oh, yeah, I got his drinking canteen, too. That's all. Just his canteen, his gun, and his belt with a little of his blood on it.

SPEAKER P

I still don't understand the way people blamed us for the war back then. We were killers, no good. Doors slammed in our faces, put down every place we went. Hell, I didn't have to go—I volunteered—wanted to fight for what I believed in. What a joke. Nobody else believed in it. But it was worth doing, even with all the crap I've had to deal with since. I've got my dignity, which is more than the draft-dodgers can say. I'm proud to call myself a Vietnam veteran. Would I do it again? Sure, every bit of it.

SPEAKER Q

Like they say, war is hell. Would I do it again? No way. Will it happen again, knowing what we know now? Sure as hell. It'll happen again and again and again.

SPEAKER R

Today we are all brothers. It don't matter what color your skin is—black, white, gray. I love all these soldiers. And I ain't too proud to admit it.

ALL

We went to war, we came home, and we *are* heroes.

PRAYER, DEDICATION AND FAREWELL

SPEAKER S

We come together today in this very sacred place to pay tribute to the brave American soldiers, sailors, airmen, and Marines who served their nation in her time of need. And at this year's Veterans Day our nation recalls in a very special way the veterans of the painful war that we've tried to forget. The veterans returning from Vietnam were not welcomed with speeches and flowers and parades as we rejoiced at the homecoming of the heroes of earlier conflicts. The Vietnam veterans returned to find demonstrations and a nation divided by an unpopular war. And now we dedicate a memorial and on its black granite walls are the names of all who have fallen in Vietnam. There are few memories more painful than those associated with the Vietnam War, yet there can be nothing more important to the heart of America that we always remember those who sacrificed so much for our country in that conflict. But we also learned a terrible lesson from that war: we learned that we should never again ask our men and women to serve in a war that we do not intend to win.

SPEAKER T

Standing before this monument we see reflected in a dark mirror dimly, and we remember ourselves, our lovers, our friends, our nation, our buddies, our families. To let go the pain, the grief, the resentment, the bitterness, the guilt. To let go of impossible dreams, old realities, lost innocence, the loss of unity, the loss of wholeness. Oh, Lord God, let the outstretched arms of this monument be your instrument of forgiveness and peace.

(Only the actor who sang the opening song and read the inscription on the monument remains. The others stand in their neat rows behind him. Simultaneously, all except him get back in their original burial positions. He is now very much alone. He begins to sing in a quavering, emotion-filled voice that rapidly grows in strength and conviction. He

sings something unashamedly patriotic, such as "God Bless America"
or "The Star-Spangled Banner." If the former is used, he should sing
through once and repeat, ending on the word "night" the second time
through the lyric. Similarly, if the national anthem is used, the play
should end this way:)

SINGER

Oh, say, can you see
By the dawn's early light
What so proudly we hailed
At the twilight's last gleaming?
Whose broad stripes and bright stars
Through the perilous fight
O'er the ramparts we watched
Were so gallantly streaming.
And the rockets' red glare,
The bombs bursting in air,
Gave proof through the night . . .

(On the last word the song ends abruptly. The lights are out. The play
is over.)

A N G E L

Angel by Jo Davidsmeyer tied for second place with *Star Dust* by Elizabeth Hemmerdinger (see Appendix). A Sarasota, Florida, computer programmer, Ms Davidsmeyer submitted an earlier draft of *Angel* to a Florida contest, and it won. It was produced there in 1987. A figurative and literal nightmare of the Nazi holocaust, *Angel* is both reminiscent of, and dramatically superior to Rolf Hochhuth's polemic dramas *The Deputy* and *Soldiers*. Though Irma Grese was worse than the monster who appears in the following pages—Isabella Leitner, a survivor of Auschwitz and author of three powerful books about the holocaust, said she saw Grese set a dog on a prisoner, who was torn to pieces, "and we were warned not to make a sound, or we would be next"—Ms Davidsmeyer's fantasy is an honest dramatization gleaned from trial records and such historical records as Olga Lengyel's harrowing biography, *The Five Chimneys*. "I don't view the Holocaust as a simple black-and-white issue," the playwright says. "I don't think it was committed by madmen. That does a disservice to the people who died. The Holocaust was executed by normal, sane people who went too far. People like Irma Grese knew what they were doing. They were everyday people and they were responsible for their actions."

The Open Book's New York production (minus projected scenery) of *Angel* opened October 27, 1994, at The Amsterdam Room with the following cast:

IRMA GRESE . . . . Kathryn Carrol
THE PROSECUTOR . . . . Jon Koons
OLGA LENGYEL . . . . Patricia Kelley
DR. JOSEPH MENGELE . . . . John Blaylock
HELENE GRESE . . . . Emily Blake
DEFENSE ATTORNEY . . . . Toby Sanders

ANGEL

A Nightmare in Two Acts

by Jo Davidsmeyer

For my sister,
Dona Davidsmeyer Beale
In eternity all questions are answered

CAST OF CHARACTERS

Irma Grese: Aged 19 to 21. Epitome of the classic nordic maiden: tall, fair, blonde, blue-eyed, and appealing. Though IRMA has never trod the boards, she is a consummate actress, able to play both saint and seductress with equal sincerity and zeal.

Olga Lengyel: Late Thirties. A Hungarian medical student interned at Auschwitz. Imprisoned, but not defeated; a survivor in every aspect.

Prosecutor: Early forties. A Major in the British army. He vainly searches for reasons in a very unreasonable world. Self-tormented by the dilemma of how a civilized society metes out justice for incomparably uncivilized acts.

Helene Grese: Aged 19, sister to IRMA. She has a simpler beauty than her sister, and a simpler nature. In the second act she assumes the role of the EXECUTIONER.

Dr. Joseph Mengele: He is a prime example of Aryan superiority, and he knows it.

Defense Attorney: A Major in the British army, self-righteous and pompous in his bigotry. About to retire.

Scenes

ACT I:
A courtroom in Lüneberg, 1945, the Belsen Trials
and
Auschwitz Concentration Camp, Spring of 1944.

ACT II:
A prison cell. Evening, December 9, 1945.
One unit set serves for all three locales.

ACT ONE

SETTING: When the audience enters, the stage is blocked by a drop unit, resembling the inside of a cattlecar with a large sliding door center. The planks of the unit do not quite meet. Harsh white light blazes through the partial openings. Occasionally, shapes can be seen passing, briefly blocking the light.

HOUSE OUT: The sounds of an approaching freight train fills the theatre. As the train comes to a halt, the sound of cattlecar doors sliding open is heard along with orders barked in a multitude of languages. The door center stage is quickly thrown open, spilling glaring hot light over the audience. Silhouetted in this light is IRMA GRESE. All noises cease abruptly.

IRMA

Welcome to Auschwitz!

(The floodlights fade to a reasonable level as IRMA steps down center into a pool of light and the drop flies out. IRMA is strikingly handsome, appearing to be the epitome of the classic nordic-maiden: tall, fair, blue-eyed and appealing. Her hair is piled high atop her head, with not a hair out of place. She wears a dark skirt, white blouse, a sky-blue jacket [specially selected by her to match her eyes] and a black string tie. A holster and pistol are strapped to her waist and a short cellophane whip is tucked inside her black top-boots. A swastika armband is proudly displayed on her right arm and S.S. insignia gleam on her collar. With the drop gone, we see that the stage is dominated by a huge red banner bearing the swastika. During IRMA's welcome speech, projections of the main gates of Auschwitz camp appear, beginning with a photo of the main gates of Auschwitz.)

You have been brought here from throughout Europe for one purpose, and one purpose alone . . . to work. Auschwitz is a work camp, as you can well see from the sign above the gates. "Arbeit macht frei"—work brings freedom! Germany needs you. Every able-bodied man, woman and child will be put to work for the glory of the Third Reich. The doctor will pass before you in order to separate you into work parties.

(The camp gates are replaced by a photo of the train selections.)

IRMA

As the doctor points to you, go in the direction he indicates and form ranks of five. If you are ill, please indicate so to the doctor. As you can well see, we have ambulances standing by to transport the sick to the camp hospital. Healthy adults will be put to work immediately. The others will be taken for showers and delousing.

(A photo of showers/gas chambers appears. The PROSECUTOR steps around the banner to watch IRMA's cheery address. He is carrying a large yellow legal pad and takes notes.)

You are being separated now, but you will all be quartered in the same camp. After work detail you will be reunited with your loved ones.

(An image of a Jewish child held at gunpoint replaces the previous photo.)

We realize that you all have been through a long and arduous journey, and many have died along the way. But that is behind you.

(The last image is of mounds of the dead awaiting their final disposition.)

You are now at Auschwitz-Birkenau. Welcome!

PROSECUTOR

Would she always greet the trains with that speech?

(OLGA LENGYEL steps from the other side of the banner. She and the PROSECUTOR bracket IRMA on both sides. IRMA continues to stare forward, oblivious to their attentions.)

OLGA

On slow days only. There was not time for their charade when shipments arrived hourly.

PROSECUTOR

And there was always a doctor present?

(MENGELE enters. He is smartly dressed in a tailored hospital coat, carrying himself as one who knows he is a prime example of Aryan superiority.)

OLGA

Yes. Often was Mengele. He liked the duty. It gave him first *choice* of the prisoners for his own purposes.

MENGELE

Irma, did you notice the finds I made today? A set of identical twins and even a dwarf. Marvelous stroke of good fortune.

IRMA

You must be very happy, Joseph.

MENGELE

My dear Irma, you might at least feign some enthusiasm.

IRMA *(crossing to him)*

I'm sorry. How are the experiments coming?

MENGELE

Quite well! The Führer has even expressed an interest in my genetic work. Finding more twins always helps, even if they are of inferior stock. And,

Angel, did I mention we've started work in sterilization? It was the Kommandant's idea. But it's quite interesting, anyway. Oh, that reminds me, I'll require some of the women from your hospital for tests. Youngsters, preferably teenagers. New outfit?

IRMA

Ja, you like it?

MENGELE

Lovely. Not as nice as the gown you wore last evening. Where do you find the time to liberate so many fine dresses?

IRMA

No use shipping all our bounty back to S.S. headquarters. There are very few size sevens in the high command.

(A train whistle blows.)

MENGELE

Another shipment. Shall we?

IRMA

I wish they would give us more warning.

(She takes a compact from her pocket to check her makeup and hair. She meticulously pats a stray hair into place.)

MENGELE

Stop fussing, Irma. You're lovely, as always. Come, your audience awaits.

(IRMA takes MENGELE's proffered arm and they begin to stroll away.)

OLGA

So meticulous. She took pains to look her best as she picked those about to die.

(HELENE enters.)

HELENE

Lies! The woman lies. My sister was not like that. I kept in contact with her all through the war. I would have known if she had done these things this liar claims. Irma is gentle, loving, always considerate. For heaven's sake, she even remembers birthdays!

IRMA

Helene? Helene, it's Irma. Happy Birthday, dearest.

HELENE

Irma? Where are you calling from? Are you back in Germany?

IRMA

No, no. I'm still in Poland.

HELENE

I don't believe it. How did you get through? The bombing raids have just about wiped out all the phone systems.

IRMA

Now a little war is not going to stop me from talking to my baby sister on a special day. Did the package arrive?

HELENE

Yes, thank you. The dress is beautiful. How did you come by a Paris gown?

IRMA

I have my ways. How are the boys? And—and how is Papa?

HELENE

He's still Papa. Nothing much changes.

IRMA

So what are you doing for your birthday? Is there a—What?—Hello?

HELENE

Irma. Are you still there?

IRMA

Yes, operator. Thank you. Helene, still on the line?

HELENE

I'm here, Irma.

IRMA

Listen, I've not much time. I might be transferred back to Germany, to Ravensbrück again. And . . . I'd like to come home. Just for a visit and if you could talk to Papa for me . . .

HELENE

Oh, Irma, after last time . . .

IRMA

I know. But maybe if you said something to him. I'd really like to come home . . .

HELENE

I don't know, Irma . . . .

IRMA

Just try, please! For me, ja?

HELENE

I'll see what I can do.

IRMA

Danke, Helene, danke. Oh, there's so much to say and not enough time. They limit our outside calls. I'm afraid I really must go. You don't know how good it's been to hear your voice. We'll see each other again, I promise.

Talk to Papa. And you give the boys a big hug from their sister.

(HELENE disappears into the shadows.)

You take care of yourself. And, well, I love you, Helene . . . Helene? Are you there? . . . Helene? . . . Aufwiedersehen.

OLGA

I'm sure she loved her family. Most beasts protect their own. But we Jews were not family. Gentle and loving? I bear scars from her tenderness.

PROSECUTOR (referring to his notes)

This was in the spring of '44?

OLGA

Yes.

PROSECUTOR

And she summoned you to her office to talk about . . .

OLGA

About Dr. Klein. She distrusted him.

IRMA

I saw you talking with Klein today, and the day before that. You two seem thick as thieves.

OLGA

We are countrymen, both from Hungary.

IRMA

Did I ask you a question? . . . So, you and he are old friends. Where did you meet?

OLGA

Here in Oswicim. I am a medical student assigned to camp hospital where Doktor Klein is in charge.

IRMA

Auschwitz, not Oswicim. I do not recognize the language you speak with him. What is it?

OLGA

Is local dialect from my region, Fräulein.

IRMA

Your name?

OLGA (surprised at the question)

Olga Lengyel.

IRMA (waves her closer with her pistol)

Well, Olga Lengyel, medical student, were you with Klein today? Did you assist him when he released the selected women from the washroom?

OLGA

Yes, Fräulein.

IRMA

I am an Arbeitsdienstführerin, Work Party Leader. I've worked long and hard to attain that prestigious title. I suggest you remember it.

OLGA

Yes, Arb—Arbeitsdienstführerin.

IRMA

Was it you who suggested Klein remove the door to the washroom? The door that I had ordered nailed shut on the women inside?

OLGA

No, no, Frau . . . Arbeitsdienstfüh—

IRMA *(loading the pistol)*

You're lying. Lengyel, you will no longer accompany Klein on his rounds. If he speaks to you, you will not answer. If he sends for you, you will not come. Understand? Good. Now let us discuss why you disobeyed me today. You didn't leave Klein and return to roll call as I ordered you to do. That's twice you have disobeyed me. Two deadly mistakes.

OLGA

Herr Doktor Klein ordered me to stay. I am a member of his infirmary staff. I thought I should obey—

IRMA

You thought? Who said you could think? Klein is merely a doctor. I am Arbeitsdienstführerin. I am to be obeyed at all times. I alone!

(She lifts OLGA's chin with the barrel of the pistol.)

Jewess, you will never disobey my orders again, nicht wahr?

OLGA

Jawohl, Arbeitsdienstführerin. Always will I obey your orders.

IRMA

See that you do.

(IRMA forces OLGA's chin up higher with the pistol.)

And so that you will remember . . . .

(IRMA slams the butt of the pistol across OLGA's face. She hauls back to begin a merciless beating, but is halted by the sudden movement of the PROSECUTOR.)

PROSECUTOR

Enough!

(He rips the banner down, revealing the full stage for the first time. It consists of five platforms which form a semi-circle around a downstage

79

*playing area which is empty except for a table set to one side. The
platforms serve as portions of a British military courtroom. Each actor
is isolated in his own area. OLGA crosses to take her place on the opposite
side of the stage from HELENE GRESE. IRMA exits. The DEFENSE
COUNSEL sits at a desk with notes arranged before him and a briefcase
at his feet. The PROSECUTOR stands before his desk. A cyclorama
surrounds the set.)*

PROSECUTOR

May it please the court, the accused are being charged with committing a
war crime, a violation of the laws and usages of war. The case for this
prosecution is simple: that at Auschwitz and Belsen a practice, a course of
conduct, had grown up under which internees were being treated in such a
way that they were of no value at all as human beings. The camp staff agreed,
either tacitly or expressly, with the course of conduct in force in the camp
to brutalize and ill-treat prisoners. This prosecution suggests that when
nationals have been put in the military machine and have been gassed and
killed without any trial, because they have committed no crime except that
of being a Jew or being unwanted by the State, that that is a clear violation
of an unchallenged rule of warfare which outrages the general sentiment of
humanity. In concluding my opening remarks, with the court's permission,
I would like to introduce the accused. One Irma Grese, aged twenty. A mass
murderess who joyed in beating defenseless, starved women; who took
pleasure in striking at those who could not strike back.

*(IRMA GRESE reenters to take her place on the center platform, in
the dock. She is now wearing a dull gray prison outfit consisting of a
skirt and blouse.)*

IRMA

My name is Irma Grese. At the age of seventeen I was made to join the S.S.
as a supervisor at concentration camps. I was aware of what was happening
at the camps and have hidden mothers and children away in order that
they should not be chosen for the gas chambers. I was once denounced by
a Jewish informer for having done this and was arrested for two days and
beaten. Conditions in the camps were bad for everyone, including the S.S.
I was told by a superior that if it was necessary I could hit prisoners, but I
never did this. I have never beaten or struck any prisoner.

PROSECUTOR

At this time the prosecution wishes to enter into evidence affidavits attesting
to acts of brutality committed by Irma Grese. Deposition of Gitla Dunkle-
man. "I was in Block II and the chief S.S. woman who dealt with us was
blonde, with her hair tied up at the back. I have been told that her name
is Irma Grese. I have personally seen this woman commit many acts of
brutality. I have seen her strike women about the face and body with a
rubber truncheon and kick them. I have seen her draw blood and knock

women senseless. She was the worst of the women S.S. Deposition of . . .

IRMA

In a previous statement I said I have never beaten or ill-treated prisoners. I have thought this over and now wish to confess that I have done so. I never struck a prisoner during the three and one-half weeks I was at Belsen Concentration Camp. However, while at Auschwitz I struck female prisoners on the face with my hand. On the whole, however, I feel that I treated prisoners quite well considering the circumstances.

(PROSECUTOR *rises with another handful of depositions. He starts to speak, but IRMA cuts him off.*)

Upon further reflection I wish to add that I have in fact, beaten prisoners other than with my hand as already described.

OLGA

My name is Olga Lengyel. I was a medical student in Hungary before I was interred at Auschwitz. That was spring of 1943. When I first saw Irma Grese, I was certain that a woman, no, a child, of such beauty could not be cruel. You look at her, and you know she was an angel. But it was soon I learn she was angel of death.

HELENE

My sister was an angel growing up. She was gentle. Not aggressive at all. When, as sometimes happens, girls were quarreling and fighting, Irma never had the courage to fight. No, she ran from violence.

OLGA

Always she carried a whip, and how she made use of it . . . and smiled at the blood and the sound of her victims' cries.

HELENE

On the farm, she could not stand even the harsh necessities of life. Often she ran into the hills on slaughtering days.

OLGA

She chose women for the slaughter. I often saw her in charge of the selections for the gas chambers.

PROSECUTOR

Explain to the court what happened during these selections.

OLGA

Selections could happen any time, at roll call, at meals, at hospital, anytime, anywhere. First selections were at the train station when prisoners arrived. Transports were divided in two groups: those fit to work and those who were not. The old, the weak, the sick, children, all were sent to the left, the gas chambers.

PROSECUTOR

The selections you witnessed in hospital, how were these handled?

OLGA

The sick, they were ordered to march naked in front of the S.S. doctors. The obviously sick were selected at once. But any small sort of thing, a bruise, cut, even mud was enough reason for selection. Always present were S.S. men and women. In particular, Irma Grese. She was also in charge of Apelle, the daily roll calls, which were often just another excuse for selections.

(PROSECUTOR sits.)

DEFENSE *(rises, crosses to IRMA)*

Miss Grese, were you ever in charge of selections for the gas chambers?

IRMA

No.

DEFENSE

What were your duties at these selections?

IRMA

As I was responsible for the women's camp, my duties included logging the number entering or leaving and I kept the figures in a strength book. Women selected from within my camp were immediately removed to Lager B and I was told that they would later be sent to another camp in Germany for special handling.

DEFENSE

Were you ever told anything about the gas chambers by your superiors?

IRMA

No. The chambers were in another part of the camp off-limits to me. I learned of them from the prisoners.

DEFENSE

You have been accused of selecting women from roll call to be sent to the gas chambers. Have you done that?

IRMA

No. How could I when I knew what would happen to them if they were selected?

DEFENSE *(to OLGA)*

Mrs. Lengyel, did any doctor whom you allege made selections for the gas chambers tell you upon what basis these decisions were made?

OLGA

No.

DEFENSE

Do you agree that your evidence as to the basis on which these selections were made is your opinion and nothing more?

OLGA

Yes.

DEFENSE

Is it not true that the persons who actually made the selections were in each and every case doctors?

OLGA

They were made by doctors in the presence of others of the camp staff.

DEFENSE

But is it not true that the S.S. personnel were present on these parades only for the purpose of control and guard?

OLGA

No. They were there, and if the doctor did not see somebody, they pointed that person out and often struck the prisoner severely.

DEFENSE

Are you aware that the S.S. doctors from time to time prepared lists of the patients who were not expected to survive their natural illnesses?

OLGA

I know not of these lists.

DEFENSE

I put it to you that the only selections made from the persons in hospital were made on the basis of such lists, without the aid of S.S. camp personnel.

OLGA

I know not of such lists. I know only what I saw. Often very, very healthy persons who were to be discharged next day were put into lines with those for the gas chambers. And often they were beaten before being taken away. More often if Grese was there.

DEFENSE *(to HELENE)*

From your knowledge of your sister, do you think her a person likely to beat prisoners under her charge?

HELENE

Never. My sister was never anything but kind and gentle. I cannot believe she would or could participate in such cruel acts. It was not even her choice to join the S.S.

IRMA

In 1938, I left the elementary school and worked six months on agricultural jobs at a farm, after which I worked in a shop in Lüchen for six months. At fifteen, I applied to become a nurse, but the Labor Exchange would not approve that and sent me to work in a dairy. In July, 1942, I again tried to become a nurse. Instead, the Labor Exchange sent me to Ravensbrück

Concentration Camp for training, although I protested against it.

DEFENSE

What happened after you completed training at Ravensbrück?

IRMA

I was allowed five days leave. I went home to visit with my family.

DEFENSE

And what transpired between you and your father during your leave?

IRMA

We argued, he beat me severely and turned me out of the house.

PROSECUTOR

When your sister was home in 1943, did you actually witness your father give her a thrashing?

HELENE

I did not see the beating, but I heard them quarrel. Papa did not approve of Irma being in the S.S.

(IRMA and her father are heard arguing. IRMA listens emotionlessly, staring intently forward.)

PAPA *(taped)*

Ausziehen es sich! Nun aber! Nimmer will ich das in meinen Haus leiden.

IRMA *(taped)*

Das ist auch mein Haus, und hier will ich das Uniform aus meinem Heimat tragen.

DEFENSE

Did he forbid her to come to the house again?

HELENE

I did not hear him say that. But Irma never came home again after that.

PROSECUTOR

You were sixteen at that time. Did you never ask your sister what she did in the camps? She never told you of her actions?

HELENE

We asked her about it, of course, but she said her work was classified and she couldn't discuss it.

PROSECUTOR

Why did your father lose his temper

PAPA *(taped)*

Nein. Ist gar nicht dein Haus! Du hast jetzt deine Heimat, aber keinem Heim.

IRMA *(taped)*

Ich Schäme mich meiner Beruf nicht! Diesmal bin ich stoltz auf meinem Beruf. Dienst Land, unsers Land.

PAPA *(taped)*

Nicht beschämt! Aber du hast deine Familie verschämt. Geh aus, Lass mich! Nun kommst nimmermehr zurück!

IRMA *(taped)*

Du kanst mir sowie nicht sprechen! Ich bin eine Deutscherbeamtin!

with her?

HELENE

Because he was very much against her
being in the S.S.

PAPA *(taped)*

Beamtin! Bist du nur ein Kind!

IRMA *(taped)*

Und Sie sind ein alter Narr!

PAPA *(taped)*

Schweig! Dirne!

IRMA *(taped)*

Wissen Sie nicht, dass ich Sie inkerk-
ern kann?

PAPA *(taped)*

Und weisst du dass ich dir jedermaleine Strafen verhängen kann? Ver-
dammenwerte Hüre!

(The sound of a slap and a stifled gasp.)

HELENE

I have not seen my father since April of 1945.

*(At the sound of another blow, IRMA shuts her eyes and the stage lights
dim except for a pinspot on her face. Behind her on the cyc appears a
photo of a whip. At the sound of the next blow, the photo dissolves into
a large shot of a whip clenched in a black-gloved fist. OLGA exits in
the dark.)*

IRMA

Nein, Vati. Bitte, nein!

(Another slap)

No. No more!

*(The photo dissolves to a larger shot of IRMA brandishing a whip in
a black-gloved fist.)*

MENGELE

(from the darkness)

Irma! . . . Irma, liebchen, it's good to see you again.

*(As IRMA opens her eyes, lights rise in the downstage playing area,
revealing MENGELE dressed in S.S. uniform. He extends his arm to
her and helps her down from the dock.)*

IRMA

Mengele? Joseph, is it you?

MENGELE

Let me look at you. You don't seem any the worse for wear.

PROSECUTOR *(from the darkness)*

Miss Grese, would you call your father a cruel man?

(IRMA whirls around, surprised at the voice. She starts to answer, but her sister answers first. Throughout this cross-examination the others are merely disembodied voices from the darkness. Photo dissolves.)

HELENE *(off)*

No, not cruel. He was very strict, though.

MENGELE

You seem to have survived your two days of confinement quite well. How did you manage?

IRMA

Would you believe me if I said it was the thought of you waiting for me that gave me strength?

MENGELE

Not for a moment.

(He and IRMA cross to a table downstage.)

DEFENSE *(off)*

As children, did you and your sister attempt to join any of the Nazi youth groups?

HELENE *(off)*

Yes. We were very anxious to become members of the Bund Deutscher Mädchen, that was Hitler's League of German Maidens.

IRMA

That's what I like about you, Mengele. You're no one's fool. It's an attractive trait.

HELENE *(off)*

But father would never allow us to join. He strictly forbade Irma and me from having any associations with the Nazi party.

MENGELE

Take off your blouse, let's have a look.

IRMA

You're usually subtler than this, dear Joseph.

MENGELE

Purely a professional interest. I was told there was some corporal punishment included in your sentence. I'm sure you've not yet had a doctor examine your back.

IRMA

Well, in the interests of medicine . . .

(IRMA removes her blouse, revealing a black camisole beneath. She sits

86

on the table with MENGELE behind her.)

DEFENSE *(off)*

Why did you wish to join Hitler's League of Maidens?

HELENE *(off)*

All the school girls were joining, all our friends were in the League. They'd tell us all about it.

PROSECUTOR *(off)*

So, though you were not members, you were still aware of the League's activities, the lessons and disciplines?

MENGELE *(lifting camisole and examining IRMA's back)*

Ah, old-fashioned German discipline. It is what makes our army great.

IRMA

Simple for you to say, Joseph. Doctors are exempt from the discipline of the cane.

MENGELE

How many strokes were you given?

IRMA

Twenty-five.

MENGELE

Not too bad.

IRMA

How would you know?

(By now, MENGELE's examining hands have worked their way from her back to her chest.)

I thought this was a purely professional examination?

HELENE *(off)*

We were very mad that our father wouldn't let us join. There was so much to do with the League: trips, picnics, professional training.

MENGELE

I'm a very thorough professional. I love my work.

(IRMA removes his hands from her body and pulls the camisole back into place.)

PROSECUTOR *(off)*

So at an early age you were both ardent young Nazis?

HELENE *(off)*

We only wanted to be doing what everyone else was.

MENGELE

Are you saving yourself tonight for our much-beloved Kommandant? Or do you prefer the Polish sausage you've been sampling?

PROSECUTOR *(off)*

Nevertheless, you were indoctrinated through your friends in their lessons of antisemitism and racial superiority.

IRMA

Liebchen, now you know I much prefer Aryans. They truly are superior in every aspect.

(She lays back on the table and pulls MENGELE down on top of her.)

Deutschland über alles.

MENGELE

Zieg heil, my angel.

(They kiss.)

PROSECUTOR *(off)*

But in later years, you never sought to join the S.S. or any other Nazi group as your sister did.

HELENE *(off)*

That is correct.

PROSECUTOR *(off)*

So, in spite of your limited exposure to Nazi propaganda at an early age, you were not driven to serve the Nazi party as your sister Irma was?

HELENE *(off)*

I was younger than Irma. She had ambitions.

IRMA *(breaking their kiss)*

Ouch!

MENGELE

What is it?

IRMA

Your medals.

MENGELE

I thought you aspired to be covered with medals?

IRMA

Covered by them, ja, but not impaled.

(As she starts to unbutton his jacket, HELENE enters downstage playing area wearing a dirndl dress, with flowers in her hair.)

HELENE

Irma! Come on, Irma. They'll be here any moment.

MENGELE

Something wrong?

IRMA

Nein . . . I . . . it's nothing.

HELENE

Are you coming down, Irma?

IRMA

Ja, Helene.

(She starts to rise, but MENGELE holds her down.)

MENGELE

Playing hard to get?

HELENE

I'm so nervous about the Festival. How can you be so calm? Oh my, I don't think I remember even the first line of the song. What are the words?

MENGELE

Can't you stay, or are you on duty tonight?

IRMA

I don't know.

HELENE

Irma, what's the first line?

IRMA

I don't know!

HELENE

What?

IRMA

I don't know . . . "Ich weiss nicht"—that's the first line.

HELENE

Ja, ja.

(Singing)

"Ich weiss nicht, was soll es bedeuten, dass ich so traurig bin . . . "

(Crossing to table.)

Irma! You're not even dressed!

(She retrieves IRMA's blouse from the floor and shakes it out. IRMA rises, but MENGELE does not let her pass by him.)

IRMA

I should check the duty roster.

HELENE *(steps around MENGELE and holds out blouse)*

Stop daydreaming. Honestly, Irma, you're always off in your own little world.

MENGELE

No, you wait here. I'll check the roster. Remember where we left off.

(He exits.)

HELENE

We've got to be leaving soon. And can't you at least be a little bit nervous, like me?

IRMA *(putting on blouse)*

Helene, you'll be wonderful. You know the song by heart and we've practiced it hundreds of times.

HELENE

I know, but . . .

IRMA

No buts. I wouldn't let my little darling sister fail. Just think of all the fun we're going to have today at the Music Festival. Everyone will be there. And this is one thing Papa can't object to.

HELENE

I'm not so sure. He complains about everything. It seems like ages since we've been to a party. And now you're going off and leaving me alone with father.

IRMA

You'll join me later, but I am not staying here one day after I graduate. I'm fifteen, I can be earning my own living. And I'm not going to miss out on any more parties or fun because Papa's so stubborn and old-fashioned. But we'll show him today. He'll see what his little girls can do.

HELENE

Don't be silly, Irma. Father's not coming. Father never goes anywhere.

IRMA

Not coming? Are you sure, Helene? I thought since we were singing . . .

HELENE

Pooh, I don't care whether he's there or not.

IRMA

I know it's silly of me, but I hoped he'd come. Well, don't you want Papa to be proud of us?

HELENE

Oh, who cares what he thinks? We're not babies any more. You're a woman about to go out in the world. What will you do when you leave?

IRMA

I'm sure I can find something through the Labor Exchange. Maybe nursing. You think I'd make a good nurse? You know there are many young, good-looking doctors in hospital. It might be fun. Or perhaps I'll become a singer or an actress. Oh, I don't know. I'll take whatever comes along, as long as it takes me away from here.

(MENGELE reenters.)

HELENE

Whatever it is, you'll be wonderful. But I'm going to miss you so much.

IRMA

Now, Helene, you have to finish school and look after the boys when I'm gone. And, ja, look after Papa, too. And when you graduate, then you come join me. It'll be just you and me and a whole world to discover. We'll dazzle them, and settle for nothing less than champagne every night.

MENGELE

Roster assigns you to corpse detail tonight. Afterwards, come to my quarters. I've just liberated a case of champagne.

HELENE

We'll do that. But for now, we've got to be going.

MENGELE

Next shift starts soon. You'd better go now.

(A gavel bangs three times.)

HELENE

To the future.

(She kisses IRMA and exits.)

MENGELE

Till then, my angel.

(He kisses IRMA and exits. IRMA stands alone and confused. Gavel sounds three more times. IRMA reluctantly exits. PROSECUTOR and DEFENSE ATTORNEY enter the downstage area.)

DEFENSE *(offering from a pack)*

Cigarette?

PROSECUTOR

Thank you.

DEFENSE

Light?

PROSECUTOR

Please.

DEFENSE

Beastly business, what?

PROSECUTOR

Yes.

91

DEFENSE

Starting the second month today.

PROSECUTOR

Really? I'd lost track of the time.

DEFENSE

Yes, yes, yes. Our two-month anniversary. That makes it a red-letter day on three counts.

PROSECUTOR

Really? Why so?

DEFENSE

My retirement's today.

PROSECUTOR

Congratulations. You'll finish out the case?

DEFENSE

Suppose I must. Wouldn't want the whole affair to start again due to my plans. But it's a bloody way to end a thirty-year career, defending a bunch of murderers and kikes.

PROSECUTOR

I believe you mean Jews.

DEFENSE

What? . . . Oh, yes, of course. I merely meant I had hoped my military career would end differently.

PROSECUTOR

You said there was a third reason to mark today?

DEFENSE

Oh, yes. Grese, it's her birthday. Twenty-one today.

PROSECUTOR

Only twenty-one? I keep forgetting she's little more than a child.

DEFENSE

And a rather dangerous one. Never forget that.

PROSECUTOR

What is she like?

DEFENSE

Grese? You have all the testimony, judge for yourself.

PROSECUTOR

That tells me of the criminal, or rather, the crimes. What of the woman?

DEFENSE

Suffice it to say, she's not the type you'd invite to high tea.

PROSECUTOR

But do you never wonder what could have made a child do such things? Look at her. Were you to meet her on the street, you'd think, "What a nice young woman!"

DEFENSE

"Nice" people don't commit murder. It's bad form.

PROSECUTOR

The world's not as simple as that.

DEFENSE

It's complex enough as is without overturning rocks to discover why vile creatures live there. Let us just get the woman tried and get on with our lives.

PROSECUTOR

The very nature of the crimes demands our attention. We can't just return to our little lives and forget.

DEFENSE

I can. I rather enjoy my little life. And I have little interest in wading through the muck to examine hers. She seems not to have. Why should I bother?

PROSECUTOR

Bother? Do you consider it a bother to try to determine what led to the slaughter of millions? We have a duty to those that are gone—

DEFENSE

Save it for the courtroom. Really, my dear boy, I wonder at the nature of this sudden interest in our lovely blonde angel.

PROSECUTOR

I've a *professional* interest, I assure you.

DEFENSE

Steady on there. I meant nothing improper.

PROSECUTOR

It's just such a fascinating case.

DEFENSE

I suppose there's a certain inherent fascination for mayhem and barbarism. It's what makes us all slow as we pass an automobile accident. But as civilized men, we never look directly at the wreckage.

PROSECUTOR

A shame. We might learn something from closer examination. If you stop to think—

DEFENSE

It's really not my place to think of anything beyond the current proceedings. Nor yours, old chap. If I were to be so bold as to make an observation, I'd say your problem is you think entirely too much. Get all muddled in minutiae.

PROSECUTOR

If you are suggesting that my handling of this case has been less than—

DEFENSE

No, no, no, old man. Nothing of the sort. Your prosecution has been flawless. You're a veritable lion before the bench. I was just offering some unsolicited advice. Be careful. Evil can be quite appealing at times, especially when it comes packaged so attractively.

PROSECUTOR

Evil? This is a young woman we're discussing, not Satan's spawn.

DEFENSE

Makes little difference. She'll hang one way or the other.

(The gavel sounds again. PROSECUTOR exits. Lights rise as DEFENSE crosses to his playing area. The courtroom is empty except for IRMA, who is perched on the Defense counsel's desk. From a pocket, she has produced a compact and lipstick and is reapplying her makeup throughout the DEFENSE's advice to her.)

DEFENSE

Now, Miss Grese, up until this time the prosecution has been light with you. They shall begin intense cross-examination today. Since incidents of beatings of prisoners by yourself have already been well established, it would be best for your case if you admit to them under my questioning, before the prosecution has a chance to—

IRMA

Is my lipstick even?

DEFENSE

If you could attend to the matter at hand. After all, it is your defense I am trying to prepare.

IRMA

What defense? We already know what the outcome will be.

DEFENSE

Naturally. I can perhaps obtain some leniency for a few of your compatriots, but for yourself there is nothing but the rope. However, in the meantime, there are procedures to be followed—

IRMA

Then you follow them. I don't need your help and I can certainly do without your arrogant self-righteousness. You have forty-five other clients to defend. Why don't you go play your little soldier games with them? I'm not interested.

DEFENSE

As you have probably already ascertained, Miss Grese, I don't really care what you do. As for myself, I have my duty to fulfill, and as disagreeable as I may find it, I will perform my assigned function to the best of my abilities. I would think that being in the S.S. you could at least appreciate that. Now you are being tried for your actions as an officer in an elite group, supposedly Germany's finest. Start behaving in a manner appropriate to your rank, and stop behaving like an insolent, ill-mannered little brat.

IRMA

How I would have loved to have had you at Auschwitz.

DEFENSE

I doubt that. I'm not a meek little lamb to be led to the slaughter.

IRMA

You misunderstand. I mean I would like to have "had" you. You might have made an amusing diversion for an evening.

DEFENSE

You would have needed a revolver.

IRMA

Only occasionally.

DEFENSE

I wouldn't think you'd be that needy.

IRMA

Danke.

DEFENSE

It wasn't meant as a compliment. I fail to see what possible pleasure could be derived from such games. A man hardly performs his best at gunpoint.

IRMA

He'd damn well better . . . Ah, finally a reaction out of you. Good. Now we can get down to business. You were about to explain what can be laughingly termed as my "defense."

DEFENSE

Just keep your answers confined to one syllable whenever possible. A simple yes or no. Nothing else!

IRMA *(saluting smartly)*

Jawohl, mein Herr! Anything else, mein Führer?

DEFENSE

The prosecution will try to have you incriminate your fellow wardresses. Say nothing about the other defendants. I will steer questions away from the camp in general. Remember, you were not responsible for conditions at the camp. They cannot blame you for the exterminations originated by your superiors.

IRMA

Ah, I was only following orders. How original!

(The gavel sounds three times. PROSECUTOR reenters and sits at his desk. DEFENSE steps downstage to deliver his remarks.)

DEFENSE

May it please the court. Before the prosecution begins its reexamination, I wish to make observations on the circumstances from which the charges arise. Whatever our personal view may be on concentration camps, they were, under German law, prisons, and the persons therein were legally imprisoned in them. The decision of the German government, which was binding on the accused, was that it was necessary for national security that these people should be detained. What was going on at Belsen and Auschwitz was beyond any one person's control. Transports streamed in daily, the camps were hopelessly overcrowded. Just due to their very numbers, the prisoners were difficult to control. In my submission, what the evidence reveals is a general standard of corporal punishment, rather than deliberate and excessive cruelty.

(He returns to his area, passing by IRMA.)

Just 'yes' or 'no' to anything he asks.

PROSECUTOR

Several witnesses in their depositions say you were the worst S.S. woman in the camp—

IRMA

Yes, they say so. They are all lying.

(DEFENSE coughs loudly.)

PROSECUTOR

You received rather rapid promotion for a young girl, did you not?

IRMA

No.

PROSECUTOR

From a dairy-girl to being in charge of 30,000 women in a matter of two years? That is fairly rapid promotion, is it not?

IRMA

No . . . not in times of war.

PROSECUTOR

Were you not specially chosen to serve in C Camp when they began the liquidation of the Hungarians?

IRMA

No.

PROSECUTOR

Were you not promoted as a reward for your services in liquidating C Camp?

IRMA

No. C Lager was not "liquidated." It was transferred to A Lager.

PROSECUTOR

And was not A Camp merely a holding area for the gas chambers?

IRMA

My, my, Major, you seem to know—

DEFENSE (whispered)

Yes or no!

IRMA

No!

PROSECUTOR

What was the function of A Camp?

(IRMA looks coquettishly at DEFENSE for permission to reply with more than a yes/no. He abjectly signals for her to continue.)

IRMA (smiling)

I do not know.

PROSECUTOR

While at C Camp did you have a dog to guard prisoners on work details?

IRMA

No.

PROSECUTOR

Dogs were trained to guard prisoners going out of camp. Did you not have one?

IRMA

No.

PROSECUTOR

Were you not allowed to have one?

IRMA

Yes.

PROSECUTOR

Then you did indeed use a dog on guard.

IRMA

No!

PROSECUTOR

Why did you not have a dog?

IRMA

Because I did not want one!

PROSECUTOR

You didn't want one. And could you always go about doing exactly as you pleased?

IRMA

Of course not.

PROSECUTOR

Let me put it to you that in fact you had a dog with you and when you were marching the work party along, the dog would round up stragglers.

IRMA

I should know better whether I had a dog or not . . .

(DEFENSE rises to intervene, sees the futility, sits down again.)

PROSECUTOR

Did you carry a stick at Auschwitz?

IRMA

Ja. An ordinary walking stick.

PROSECUTOR

Did you also carry a whip, as witnesses claim?

IRMA

Ja. It was made in the camp weaving factory.

PROSECUTOR

What kind of whip was it?

IRMA

A very light whip.

PROSECUTOR

But it was effective when used on prisoners.

IRMA

If used on someone, it would hurt.

PROSECUTOR

Were any camp orders issued regarding whips?

IRMA

Ja.

PROSECUTOR

What were these orders?

IRMA

Eight days after they were in use, Kommandant Kramer prohibited whips in the camp.

PROSECUTOR

Did you continue carrying your whip after receiving orders against their use?

IRMA

Ja.

PROSECUTOR

I suggest that you thought it quite clever to have a whip designed for your use and that even when the Kommandant ordered you to stop using it, you went on, did you not?

IRMA

Ja.

PROSECUTOR

What was the whip really made of?

IRMA

Cellophane paper. It was plaited like a pigtail and translucent, like white glass. It was quite a lovely thing. We had fine craftsmen in the camp.

PROSECUTOR

Was it the type of whip one would use on a horse?

IRMA

It was similar.

PROSECUTOR

Did the other wardresses have these whips made as well?

IRMA

No.

PROSECUTOR

It was just your bright idea?

IRMA

Yes.

PROSECUTOR

While at C Camp, you would also carry a walking-stick, and sometimes would beat prisoners with the whip and sometimes the stick?

IRMA

I never carried both at once, it was too awkward to handle.

PROSECUTOR

Were you ever directly ordered to beat prisoners under your charge?

IRMA

No.

PROSECUTOR

So it was not a question of having orders from your superiors to be so armed. You in fact did this against orders, did you not?

IRMA

Ja.

PROSECUTOR

Were you the only person who beat prisoners against regulations?

IRMA

I do not know.

PROSECUTOR

Did you ever see any of the other accused beat prisoners?

IRMA

I was not tasked with keeping track of my fellow wardresses.

PROSECUTOR

When other warders were assigned to work under you, did you ever order them to beat prisoners?

IRMA

Ja.

PROSECUTOR

Had you the right to issue such orders?

IRMA

Not specifically.

PROSECUTOR

You affected heavy top-boots and you liked to walk round with a revolver strapped on your waist and a whip in your hand, did you not?

IRMA

No, I did not like it.

PROSECUTOR

Gertrude Diament in her deposition said that your favorite habit was to beat women until they fell to the ground and then kick them as hard as you could with those heavy top-boots of yours.

IRMA

That is a lie. Perhaps it is her habit to lie.

PROSECUTOR

Do you recall the incident when a mother was trying to talk to her daughter across the wire, and you beat the woman until she fell bleeding to the ground?

IRMA

No.

PROSECUTOR

Have you regularly beaten so many women that you cannot recollect whether it happened or not?

IRMA

I do not remember the incident. And I did not beat so many women that I would not be able to remember.

PROSECUTOR

The witness Ilona Stein spoke of an incident when you kicked her. I suggest that you regularly indulged in brutalizing prisoners assigned to your care, and that it was all part and parcel of this business of swaggering about in top-boots.

IRMA

I would like to know who has seen me swaggering in the camp. I have never kicked anyone—with boots or without. And I would like to ask you to leave out this word "regularly."

PROSECUTOR

Did you regularly carry your whip at Belsen and Auschwitz?

IRMA

Nein. I regularly kept it tucked in my top-boots. The ones I have regularly been accused of swaggering about in.

DEFENSE

Were your jackboots issued to you with your uniform, and did all the wardresses at Auschwitz wear them?

IRMA

Yes.

DEFENSE

Was the revolver also regular issue, and were you ordered to wear it?

IRMA

Yes, we were told it was for protection against partisans.

DEFENSE

And the whip, was that also for self-protection?

IRMA

No, it was to maintain discipline.

PROSECUTOR

I suggest that by the time you were transferred to Belsen, these sadistic acts had become an integral part of your life. So much so that when offered transfer, you asked to be allowed to stay at Belsen to continue your conduct right up to the time that you knew the British would be liberating the camp.

IRMA

My request to stay had nothing whatsoever to do with my work in the camps.

PROSECUTOR

Then why did you elect to stay at Belsen?

IRMA

It was for quite a different reason.

PROSECUTOR

What was that reason?

IRMA

It was a private affair.

DEFENSE

Answer the question, Miss Grese.

IRMA

I became acquainted with an S.S. man while at Auschwitz who was also transferred with me to Belsen. He is the reason I wanted to stay.

(HELENE and OLGA enter from opposite sides of the stage.)

PROSECUTOR

Were you lovers?

IRMA

Ja.

(During the next two speeches, PROSECUTOR remains by IRMA, unable to remove his eyes from her.)

HELENE

We were raised in a religious home. Father made sure that church was an important part of our lives. We both sang in the choir. Irma has a lovely singing voice, a bright, clear soprano . . . She is no murderer! She is a God-fearing woman and has always behaved in a way to bring honor to our family. I grew up admiring my sister.

OLGA

Somehow we both hated and admired her. So beautiful she was, even when she moved among us laying the whip. We couldn't comprehend someone

102

so beautiful being so cruel.

(PROSECUTOR is mesmerized by IRMA's eyes. He takes a few steps back from her to begin his questioning of OLGA, but never removes his eyes from IRMA.)

PROSECUTOR

While at Auschwitz, did you perform any personal medical services for Irma Grese?

OLGA

Yes.

PROSECUTOR

Of what nature?

OLGA

I performed an abortion.

PROSECUTOR

If you will, please describe to the court how Irma Grese solicited your services.

(Lights fade on all but OLGA and downstage playing areas.)

OLGA

She came to me in hospital one day. I thought it was to be another selection. But she sent away all the patients, leaving me alone with her.

(IRMA enters downstage area. She wears her S.S. uniform cape.)

IRMA

I have been told you're very clever. I require your services. Some minor corrective surgery.

OLGA

It was a very difficult situation she put me in. Very, very dangerous it was to refuse her anything. Yet if her superiors found out about the illegal operation both of us would be in grave danger. When I hesitated, she tried to bribe me.

IRMA

It's a simple operation. And you will be rewarded for your effort. I can be quite generous. I could share my breakfast with you one morning. You will have either wonderful chocolate or perhaps real coffee with milk. Think of it, real coffee.

OLGA

But the danger . . .

IRMA

Cakes, too, and bread with butter!

103

OLGA

If anyone found out . . .

IRMA

I will also give you a winter coat, very warm and thick. It would make you the wealthiest woman in this camp.

OLGA

Please, Fräulein, I cannot.

IRMA *(draws revolver)*

No, you can. And you will. You have no choice.

OLGA

I took her then into the operating room. That was the first time I ever saw her without her air of composure. This time it was she who was afraid. Through the procedure, she never once dropped the pistol. Strange, the thing most I remember, that was the only time I ever saw her hair out of place.

> *(IRMA crosses to OLGA and reaches a hand up to her on the platform. But OLGA just stares at it in remembered horror. IRMA drops the hand and signals with the pistol for her to step down. Loath to reenter the nightmare, OLGA must be convinced with a nudge of the pistol. When the two women are both down on the same level, IRMA sits on the table.)*

We should start now.

IRMA

Are you in such a rush to kill a German child?

OLGA

Of course not.

IRMA

Do not think you can use this opportunity to be rid of me. I swear if you try anything, I'll have you thrown to the dogs. Perhaps you've heard what the guards have trained them to do with female prisoners? Or maybe Mengele's experiments. You know what he does in that lab of his, don't you? . . . Will it hurt?

OLGA

There's no danger.

IRMA

Then why am I so scared?

OLGA

Lie back. It will be over soon.

> *(PROSECUTOR enters scene, remaining in background, observing.)*

PROSECUTOR

What happened after the operation was completed?

OLGA

I stayed with her until she was well enough to go. She talked with me a while, forgetting for a moment I was an insignificant prisoner. She even let go of the gun. Very talkative she was, almost as if chatting with a friend.

IRMA *(lighting a cigarette)*

Cigarette?

OLGA

Thank you, no.

IRMA

Take it. It's not poisoned.

OLGA *(taking cigarette)*

Thank you, Fräulein.

IRMA *(gently)*

Arbeitsdienstführerin, remember?

OLGA

I remember.

IRMA

Thank you . . . for not killing me. Though perhaps you should have. Why do I feel guilty about the one little it—thing that was inside me?

OLGA

It was a girl.

IRMA

A girl? I had a daughter? . . . Damn you! Why did you have to tell me? A girl? Oh, she might have been so lovely. They say I'm quite attractive. Do you think so?

OLGA

You're beautiful.

IRMA

A girl. Do you realize, Olga, that between us we have committed a capital offense? We have killed one of the master race; while our beloved Führer is actually paying young German women to create as many Aryans as possible. Ja, they even get a medal for the supreme service to the Fatherland of producing many beautiful, superior Aryans. And we've just killed one. You and me. Hitler would have paid a good price for my little girl. Pure Aryan heritage, with parents so beautiful and so proud. Fine examples of the master race. She would have been so lovely. How old?

OLGA

Probably three months.

105

IRMA

So young to have never lived. A daughter . . . Do you have children, Olga?

OLGA *(surprised at the question)*

Yes—no! No, I had two sons. Both were sent to the gas chambers.

IRMA

Olga, you've been listening to idle chatter. We don't have gas chambers here. Officially, they are bakeries.

OLGA

Why, then, my sons are alive and baking bread, along with my parents. And I, I who brought them here, still live.

IRMA

You brought them here?

OLGA

Oh, yes. We weren't arrested. We came willingly. It was my husband who was arrested. No, not really. We were told his services as a doctor were needed in Germany.

IRMA

A plausible lie.

OLGA

Oh, yes. And the German officials were so very, very considerate. I was so upset at my husband being sent away. and they kindly allowed me to go with him. You see, they had no wish to separate families. Arrangements could be made, for a price.

IRMA

You paid them to send you here?

OLGA

I wanted to be with him. I thought everything would be fine as long as we stayed together.

IRMA

Go on.

OLGA

My parents tried to change my mind, but I was going. Then—then they decided to come with us as well. Things were bad at home. We were the fortunate ones, we were going where we were needed, while our friends were being arrested, or just disappeared into the night. So we left, accepting the hospitality of the German officials: me, my husband, mama and papa and my two sons.

IRMA

Why do you all insist on making it so easy for us?

OLGA

I suppose we did. We learned soon enough, on the train. A train ride from Hungary to Germany via Hell. Ninety-six people forced into a car built to hold eight horses. There wasn't even enough room for all to sit down at one time. Two died the first night. We cried out for them to remove the bodies, but no one answered. Five days we traveled in that car, with the dead piling up around us, no food, we got water only once. We traded all our jewelry with a soldier for one helmetful of water. But before he handed it inside, he pissed in it. And there was smallpox in the car, and typhus, and diseases without name. When the train finally stopped, oh, so very certain were we that now would come relief. We were wrong, weren't we, Arbeitsdienstführerin?

(IRMA just stares in horrified fascination, having never heard the familiar story from this viewpoint.)

We even had to spend another night in the car.

IRMA

Sometimes shipments back up . . . we get behind and . . . well, you know better than I.

OLGA

Yes, so I do. The next day we were processed. And then—then I killed my family. Believed, I did, your story about children and the old ones being cared for. The doctor sent my youngest boy to the left, to the line for the gas chambers . . . Sorry, I should say bakeries. The doctor paused at Arvad, my eldest. Thinking I was saving him from hard work, I told the doctor my son was not yet twelve, too young for hard labor.

IRMA

My God!

PROSECUTOR *(overlapping with IRMA)*

My God!

OLGA

And then I saw my Arvad sent to join the old and young at the left. So happy at such kindness from the doctor, I dared to speak again to plead for my mother, saying she should go with my sons, to take care of them. And doctor, so kind, smiled he did and sent her with my sons to—

IRMA

Shut up! I don't want to hear about your damned Jewish family . . . Olga, don't you know? You're vermin. Ja, you're filth! You're a blight that must be purged from the face of Europe. I have it on the best authority. I don't want to know that you're a person, that you are a *woman who has loved and been loved* . . . Don't you see? You're not supposed to be!

OLGA

Of course, Arbeitsdienstführerin.

(Rushing from her, IRMA speaks tenderly to the child that is no longer part of her.)

IRMA

My little daughter, you had the seed of greatness in you. You could have done anything you wanted, been anything you wanted to be. But no more, no more . . . Have another cigarette, Olga.

(When OLGA hesitates, IRMA flings the pack at her.)

Take it, dammit! Take the whole pack . . . Do you think she would have had my eyes? She might have been . . . Did you know I wanted to be an actress? Ja! I thought that would be so grand. When I worked at hospital, they said I had the looks for it. I would have loved that. I always liked play-acting. Sometimes, that's all there is. After the war, when all this is over, maybe I'll go into pictures. You will see my name in lights, Olga. Who knows? My experiences might prove useful to me in my artistic career. To perform, to be anyone in the world, to create a beautiful image. Acting you can be anybody, do anything. For a flickering moment, you can be greater than yourself, be something different from yourself, better, more beautiful.

OLGA

Instead, you are here.

IRMA

Ja. Instead I am here . . . Finish your cigarette, Jew. Then report to the gas chambers. You're expected.

(MENGELE's whistling is heard offstage. The women and PROSECUTOR turn toward him as he enters. He is now wearing a tailored hospital coat.)

OLGA

Herr Doktor!

IRMA

Joseph, what are you doing here?

MENGELE

I work here. Come along, Jew. I have need of trained medical personnel. For the present, I cannot allow talent to be wasted in the ovens.

IRMA

This is camp business, Mengele. This Jew is one of my prisoners, she is not assigned to your staff. Don't interfere.

MENGELE

Oh, our little Mama's getting upset.

IRMA

How dare you! Did she tell you?

OLGA

No, no! I tell no one!

MENGELE *(takes IRMA in his arms)*

Now, now, little Mama.

IRMA

Don't call me that, and keep your hands off me.

MENGELE

I will place my hands where I wish, and I will call you what you are, or rather, what you were. No use in disposing of this creature to keep secret what is common knowledge.

> *(IRMA breaks from MENGELE's grasp. She dives for the pistol that she left on the examining table. Before she can level it, he grabs her wrist in a painful grip, forcing it back until she drops the weapon. He slaps her face, sending her sprawling to the floor. Without thinking, PROSECUTOR rushes to her side, stopping himself just in time before he makes a fool of himself by offering comfort to IRMA. MENGELE nonchalantly retrieves the pistol, dusts it off and puts it in his pocket.)*

MENGELE

Temper, temper! I love what your eyes do when you're playing at righteous indignation.

IRMA

Get out of here!

MENGELE

I'm disappointed, Liebchen, that you did not consult me regarding the child. Don't you think I should have been consulted?

IRMA

Why would I tell you?

MENGELE

You mean to say . . . Well, it matters little now. Pity, Daddy would have been so pleased. But now we'll never be sure if there might have been another heir to the Mengele fortune, will we?

IRMA

Oh, but I am quite sure. It's you who will always wonder.

MENGELE

Ah, little Mama, I never wonder about things of no consequence. Now why don't you go put on that pretty new dress you liberated and we'll have a wonderful supper in my quarters. You can fix it.

IRMA

Herr Doktor Mengele, the only time I wish to be with you is at selections, when I have my pistol and whip firmly in hand.

109

MENGELE *(to OLGA)*

You, come along before Mama throws another tantrum.

(OLGA exits. MENGELE starts to leave, but pauses.)

By the way, we've had wonderful success at the laboratory with our sterilization experiments. We could add your name to the list.

(MENGELE exits. IRMA pounds the floor in impotent rage. PROSECUTOR kneels down beside her.)

PROSECUTOR

Irma?

(Full stage lights return abruptly. HELENE and OLGA have returned to their places. HELENE is reading from a magazine, quite upset. MENGELE is seated casually on one of the desks, unnoticed by the others.)

DEFENSE

How old were you at the time?

IRMA

I was nineteen.

PROSECUTOR

Only nineteen?

IRMA

Ja. But old enough.

(PROSECUTOR once more falls prey to IRMA's mesmerizing eyes. HELENE begins to quietly weep. Curious, MENGELE reads over her shoulder.)

MENGELE

Irma! You've finally made it. *Life* magazine. Oh, stop sniveling, you silly little bitch. This is the big time. "Testimony of ex-prisoners painted Irma Grese as a woman who in her short life has surpassed the most blood-curdling murderesses and sadists of previous history. With her riding crop, Irma Grese ferociously beat women prisoners to the ground."

HELENE

No.

MENGELE

"She tied together the legs of women in childbirth, so that they were unable to deliver and died in great—"

(HELENE rushes off, crying. MENGELE picks up magazine and wanders down to IRMA.)

Stunning photo. Where was I? Yes—". . . died in great agony. Irma's codefendants all showed signs of terror. But Irma's face moved only once. Then it was to laugh."

110

(He tries to show the magazine to IRMA, but she has eyes only for PROSECUTOR.)

Yes, I see. Not laughing now, are we?

DEFENSE

Are you quite through with your cross-examination? . . . Major!

PROSECUTOR

Didn't you realize that people were dying all around you?

IRMA

Of course I realized it.

(She reaches out to touch his cheek. PROSECUTOR rises and finally gets back into his questioning.)

PROSECUTOR

Let me put this finally to you. Your sister said that when you were a little girl you were frightened to stand up for yourself . . .

(As IRMA rises, PROSECUTOR's resolve waves.)

. . . and that you ran away to avoid a fight. I now suggest to you that you found it great fun to hit somebody who could not hit back.

IRMA

Nein.

PROSECUTOR

I suggest that you enjoyed brutalizing helpless women.

IRMA *(backing him up)*

And I suggest that you cannot even begin to imagine what it was like at Auschwitz, and that you cannot have the slightest idea of what was going on in my mind.

PROSECUTOR *(retreating from her advance)*

I suggest that you went into the concentration camp service a frightened young girl, according to your sister, a cowardly little girl, and found yourself for the first time in a position to strike people when they could not strike back.

IRMA

Ja, it might have been that I was frightened as a child, but I grew up in the meantime.

(PROSECUTOR has no further room to escape. For the first time, IRMA touches him and all action freezes except for MENGELE, who crosses down to the two of them.)

MENGELE *(laughing)*

My, my, my.

(He exits whistling his persistent aria.)

BLACKOUT

ACT TWO

SETTING: A British prison camp inside Germany. Evening, December 9, 1945. The stage lights rise to reveal the confines of a prison cell with sandbags and barbed-wire in the distance. Shadows of cell bars cut across the stage. The cell is furnished with a bed, nightstand, a chair, and a small shelf that holds a makeup case and a hand-mirror. On the nightstand is a metal pitcher and several tin cups. The only decoration is a sprig of mistletoe suspended from the center of the cell. There is a prisoner huddled asleep in the bed, with back to the audience. IRMA is pacing about the cell. HELENE is seated down right, outside the cell. She is reading aloud from a prayerbook.

HELENE

Out of the deep have I called unto thee, O Lord; Lord, hear my voice. O let thine ears consider well the voice of my complaint. If thou, Lord, wilt be extreme to mark what is done amiss, who may abide it?

(As HELENE reads, an image of a scaffold comes into focus on the cyclorama. Distantly, military drums begin a persistent beat.)

For there is mercy with thee; therefore shalt thou be feared. I look for the Lord; my soul doth wait for him; in his word is my trust. My soul fleeth unto the Lord before the morning watch.

(The drums pick up in intensity.)

IRMA

Not yet!

(The scream abruptly halts the drums.)

HELENE

Yea, before the morning watch.

IRMA

It's not time yet!

(The image fades.)

HELENE

What did you say, Irma?

112

IRMA

Not time yet. Save your prayers 'til after I'm gone.

HELENE

There's still time. Irma, won't you pray with me? The Lord is merciful. Even after all that has passed, if you would lay your sins before him, take him into your heart—

IRMA

Oh, please, Helene! Can't we just talk? Maybe share a few laughs? It's in the Bible, Helene. Let us eat, drink and be merry, for tomorrow . . . You're angry with me. Please don't be. Not tonight. Especially not tonight.

HELENE

I just wish you wouldn't make jokes about it.

IRMA

Why? Because I'm going to be hung tomorrow? Best time I can think of for gallows humor.

HELENE

I'm sure you're more familiar with that than I am . . . Here, I brought the papers you asked for.

IRMA *(takes newspapers)*

My, my! Made the headlines again! "Blonde Angel of Auschwitz Dies Tomorrow." Top billing! The others being hung barely get a mention. It seems I'm famous.

HELENE

Infamous.

IRMA

You always said I'd be big news someday.

HELENE

This wasn't quite what I had in mind.

(IRMA settles into chair to read the papers as HELENE returns to her prayerbook.)

Man, that is born of woman, hath but a short time to live, and is full of misery. He cometh up, and is cut down, like a flower. In the midst of life we are in death. O Lord God most holy, O holy and most merciful Savior, deliver us not into the bitter pains of eternal death. As our Savior Christ hath taught us, we are bold to say, Our Father who art—

IRMA

Our father . . . he won't come, will he?

(HELENE shakes her head.)

You talked with him? Told him I asked to see him? . . . I see. And the boys? What of them? Won't either of my brothers even come to say good-bye?

113

(HELENE remains silent.)

Is it because Papa won't let them, or—or don't they want to see me again? . . .
Answer me!

HELENE

I've made arrangements for the funeral. If you approve, I'll—

IRMA

I don't give a damn what you do with my body! They won't come, will they?

HELENE

No.

IRMA

And you? My dear, dear sister, you really don't want to be here either,
do you? You don't even want to be in the same room with me any more.
Helene . . .

> *(IRMA reaches to take her sister's hand, but HELENE rises out of her
> reach. After a moment, HELENE notes the only decoration in the cell.)*

HELENE

That's new. Mistletoe?

IRMA

What? . . . Oh, ja. Well, with Christmas coming I thought we could use a
little cheer. I think I meant it as a joke at the time.

HELENE

Haven't we had enough of your jokes?

IRMA

Do you hate me?

HELENE

Don't be absurd.

IRMA

Absurd of me, of course! It's not proper to hate your sister. And you always
do the proper thing, don't you?

HELENE

I try.

IRMA

Indeed you do. Testifying at the trial, performing the proper number of
prison visits. Fulfilling your sisterly duty, whether you want to or not.
Upholding the family honor!

HELENE

It was my Christian duty.

IRMA

Honor and duty. That at least I can understand. It's what we swore to.

Honor and duty to the Reich! My, what a wonderful little Nazi you would have made.

(HELENE crosses to exit.)
Will you be there tomorrow?

HELENE

At the hanging?

IRMA

Ja.

HELENE

No! Unlike you, Irma, I have no desire to . . . No, I won't be there.

IRMA

Oh, but isn't that part of the role of the faithful sister? Standing at my side to the bitter end, nobly bearing the shame and disgrace—

HELENE

Let's not talk about it. I've consulted with a local minister. His church has a small cemetery—

IRMA

No. Just burn me and have done with it. I think that's fitting.

HELENE

Poetic justice, some would say.

IRMA

Yes, I rather like that. Scatter the ashes wherever you want. It'll be easier that way. I wouldn't want you to feel obliged to make dutiful little visits to the cemetery once a year.

HELENE

Thank you, yes. I think that would be best. I shall pray for you, Irma. Before I go, won't you pray with me, just once?

IRMA

Oh, will you stop hiding behind your prayerbook! I know you think you're doing the right thing. But I'd really just rather talk.

HELENE

There's nothing to be said. I'm tired, Irma. Tired of it all. I just want it to be over.

IRMA

And that's all?

HELENE

Yes, that's all. Shall we pray? I believe in God the Father—

IRMA

I don't want your damned prayers! I want my sister. I want to talk with you.

115

To know what you think of me. If you still can love me after all this. I want the truth!

(IRMA *violently knocks the prayerbook out of HELENE's hands.*)

HELENE

The truth! Do you really want the truth? To hear that I can't stand the sight of you? That you disgust me? I look at you and get ill! Is that what you want to hear? The truth? The real truth is that you are not my sister!

(HELENE *quickly calms herself and collects her things, putting on her cloak and veiled hat.*)

No. I knew my sister. And I loved her very much. But you couldn't possibly be her. You see, she died. I'm not really sure when it happened, but it was a very long time ago. I mourn her loss. She was so tender, so loving. So much talent that just went to waste. It was such a shame.

IRMA

My God, don't do this to me, Helene. What happened had nothing to do with you and me. What I did can't change what we had together. For God's sake, won't you look at me! I'm still your sister. In spite of everything, I'm still Irma.

HELENE *(inspects her sister)*

I'm sorry, but I don't know you.

(IRMA *grabs HELENE's hand. HELENE screams and breaks from her grasp.*)

Don't touch me! You're not human. You're just some . . . some filthy, bloody beast.

(HELENE *exits.*)

IRMA

Helene, wait. Helene!

(IRMA *stares after her for a beat. For lack of anything else to do, she sits at the table and reapplies her lipstick. Staring questioningly at her reflection, she lets the lipstick drop.*)

Filthy, bloody beast . . . Beast. Barbarian. Animal.

(IRMA *slams the mirror down on the table.*)

No. I do not choose to be a beast tonight. I will be something else. I can be anything I want to be.

(*Starts prowling nervously about the cell.*)

Let's see now, what do I want to be this evening? I could be a—a dancer! Yes, a few turns across the floor. One-two-three, one-two-three . . . or maybe a circus performer, walking the high-wire. Dazzling the crowds! No, no, no. That's not it. What I want to be tonight—what I want to be is . . . free.

(*Stops her frenetic activity and sinks to the floor.*)

Free. Now there's something I haven't been in years. God, this place reminds me of Auschwitz. My room was just like this. Same size, same cot, same moth-eaten blankets, even the same view. Only difference is the prisoners are better fed.

(Leaps up and crosses to the table to fix her hair. Picks up mirror again.)
Filthy beast, huh? Well, you may be a beast, but at least you'll be the best looking beast in the cell block. Even if you are a barbarian.

MENGELE

Of course you're a barbarian.

(He steps out of the shadows onto the platform.)
We're all barbarians. The Führer said so himself. Hello, my angel. Here we are again, just like old times. Though I must admit I rather pictured you in a gilded cage, not a barbed-wired one.

IRMA

Joseph, must you always haunt my nightmares?

MENGELE

Oh, Liebchen, this isn't *your* nightmare.

IRMA

Go away, Mengele. I do not choose to imagine you tonight.

(MENGELE starts whistling.)
I said go away! Now. I'm dismissing you from my mind. Poof! Vanish!

MENGELE

Oh, you are amusing at times, my dear. Come now, Irma, enough of this boring self-pity. Chin up, head high, you've a reputation to maintain. You are the blonde angel of Auschwitz. You're international news! It's what you've always wanted.

IRMA

Right now I'd prefer to do without the attention.

MENGELE

Nonsense! Irma, you thrive on attention. You require it, like others require air.

IRMA

Go away.

MENGELE

But then, my dear, you'd be all alone with yourself. What on earth would you do?

IRMA *(indicates the inmate asleep on the cot)*
I have my fellow inmates for company.

MENGELE

Well, I'll admit you've a captive audience. But hardly an enthusiastic one. Don't you think it's time we woke him?

(MENGELE roughly kicks the cot, jarring awake the prisoner, who tosses the blanket aside, revealing himself to be the PROSECUTOR.)

Wake up! You wouldn't want to miss anything.

PROSECUTOR

What's happening? Where am I?

MENGELE

Not very original, is he?

(The PROSECUTOR is very confused and agitated. He moves about the cell, looking for a way out.)

Not really your kind, dear. You should have elected a better crowd to be hung with. Not this disreputable group of yids and commoners.

IRMA

Well, the members of the Auschwitz aristocracy were notable in their absence from the trial.

MENGELE

Ah, yes. Daddy's very good at arranging things.

PROSECUTOR

What is happening here? I demand to be told what is happening.

IRMA

Don't ask me. It's your nightmare.

MENGELE

No, no, no. This is all wrong. You should have arisen and proclaimed, "I suppose you're wondering why I've called you here." Would you like to try again?

PROSECUTOR

This can't be happening! This isn't real.

MENGELE

Of course it's not real. You're not paying attention! This is a nightmare.

IRMA

Which would make me the woman of your dreams.

PROSECUTOR

Enough! I'm going to wake up now.

MENGELE

Oh, I don't think so. You took a sleeping pill, remember? You could try pinching yourself.

IRMA

Here, let me.

PROSECUTOR

NO! Stay away from me.

MENGELE

Is that any way to behave? Now be a good little Major and play along. You must play out the scene. That's why you've summoned us. That's why you've come.

IRMA

You've come for the show.

MENGELE

And we'll not disappoint you. Let's set the scene. Lights, please! Danke. Some background music. Perhaps some prisoners singing.

IRMA

Something bawdy and off-key.

(*Female voices are heard singing "In Munchen Steht Ein Hofbrauhaus."*)

MENGELE

Ah, yes, that will do nicely. Irma, down right at the makeup table. Major over here, as if you've just entered the cell.

(*PROSECUTOR is in a daze and allows himself to be maneuvered by MENGELE.*)

No, that's not quite right. Ah, I know what's missing. You look unclothed without your briefcase. Props!

(*A briefcase is lowered into the cell. MENGELE unhooks it from the wire and places it in the PROSECUTOR's hand.*)

Perfect! Now we're ready to enact your dreams. Irma! Look a bit more flustered that the Major has decided to pay you a visit. Very good. Now, go!

(*IRMA instantly becomes believably meek and vulnerable.*)

IRMA

You came.

(*MENGELE has to nudge PROSECUTOR to get him into the scene.*)

PROSECUTOR

You asked me to.

IRMA

So I did.

MENGELE

Your line.

119

PROSECUTOR

You . . . you wrote—wrote me a letter. That's right, you wrote and asked to see me . . . but I never answered.

IRMA

You've answered now. But it wasn't I who wanted to see you. No, the other way around.

PROSECUTOR

What?

IRMA

You wanted to come, wanted to talk with me. To ask me something. And, frankly, I wanted to know what it was that so troubled you all through the trial.

PROSECUTOR

So, now you're a mindreader.

IRMA

Don't flatter yourself. You have a terrible stud face . . . Isn't that the right colloquialism?

MENGELE

I believe the phrase is "poker face."

IRMA

Ah, poker face. Anyway, I don't see how you've survived as a prosecutor. Your emotions are so very transparent. It's most interesting watching the conflicting thoughts flash across your features. During the trial most of the time I would just sit and watch you.

PROSECUTOR

And what did you see?

IRMA

Questions and . . . no, I shouldn't say.

PROSECUTOR

Yes?

IRMA

I was probably mistaken.

PROSECUTOR

Oh, you are good. I'll admit that. You're very good at manipulating people into asking the right questions. The dramatic line, the well-timed pause. "Questions and . . . no!"

MENGELE

Careful, Irma, he's on to you.

120

PROSECUTOR

Stop your games. You were saying, questions and . . .

IRMA

Guilt.

(No reaction from PROSECUTOR)

Well, then, to the questions.

PROSECUTOR *(opens briefcase, removes notes)*

Yes. We have received information that you have been secretly in communication with Mengele.

IRMA

Mengele?

PROSECUTOR

Have you been in contact with him?

MENGELE

What an absurd accusation. I have better things to do with my time.

IRMA

Who plays games now? This is not what you came to find out.

PROSECUTOR

Will you answer the question? What are you smiling at?

IRMA

If you insist on interrogating me, I wish you wouldn't do it while standing under the mistletoe.

(He ignores her attempt at levity, takes a step downstage.)

PROSECUTOR

Mengele. Have you been in contact with him?

IRMA

No. I have not seen or heard from Mengele since we were together at Auschwitz-Birkenau.

PROSECUTOR

Do you know where he is hiding?

IRMA

No. But it is an excellent question. Well, darling?

MENGELE

Oh, just traveling abroad, enjoying the good life.

PROSECUTOR

Many S.S. wanted for questioning are still at large. Did you know of any escape plans to smuggle S.S. out of the country?

IRMA *(taking a cigarette)*

Obviously not.

PROSECUTOR

There are some questions I have about Auschwitz and the—

IRMA

Do you have a light?

PROSECUTOR

Sorry, no.

MENGELE

Try your breast pocket.

(Much to his surprise, the PROSECUTOR withdraws a lighter from his pocket. With cigarette in hand, IRMA crosses to him. She does not take the proffered lighter, but waits for him to light the cigarette for her. She leans in close to him to inhale, but he immediately backs away.)

IRMA

You were saying?

PROSECUTOR

Did you assist in Mengele's experiments?

IRMA

Ja.

MENGELE

Actually, she was little aid. However, she was an attractive ornament to have about.

PROSECUTOR

You always denied being in charge of work parties outside the camp. Did you supervise prisoners on work parties?

IRMA

Ja.

PROSECUTOR

Did you select prisoners for the gas chambers?

IRMA

Ja.

PROSECUTOR

Did you set your dog to attack prisoners?

IRMA

Nein.

PROSECUTOR

What?

MENGELE

That means no.

PROSECUTOR

Will you be quiet!

MENGELE

There's no need to raise your voice to me. After all, I'm only a figment of your imagination. If you're tired of me, simply command me to vanish, and I'll be gone.

PROSECUTOR

Really? In that case . . . Bugger off!

MENGELE

Well! Testy, aren't we?

(*MENGELE exits.*)

IRMA

Alone, at last!

PROSECUTOR

Miss Grese, you did not have your dog attack the prisoner Rosenwayg, as was testified to at the trial?

IRMA

No, I did not.

PROSECUTOR

You're lying, aren't you?

IRMA

No.

PROSECUTOR

No?

IRMA *(smiling)*

No.

PROSECUTOR

Really?

IRMA

Really. Major, I'm dying tomorrow at ten o'clock. Why should I lie?

PROSECUTOR

Oh.

IRMA *(laughing)*

Major, I cannot stand dogs. They frighten me, they always have.

(Her simple merriment is contagious; he smiles as well.)

I knew it. You have a very pleasant smile, Major. This is the first time I've seen the lines of a smile break through that stodgy British decorum. Surely it's not dogs and Auschwitz that make you smile.

PROSECUTOR

Your laughter, it's pleasant. And damned if it isn't innocent and girlish. That was the only ray of sunshine in the months of proceedings, that one time you laughed.

IRMA

God, that was *so* stupid of me! But it *was* funny! Certainly enough happened at Belsen and Auschwitz, that woman did not have to invent a horror story. And such a blatant lie.

PROSECUTOR

I know. I could have shot the lieutenant who screened her testimony. You should have seen the report I wrote on that little incident . . .

(He stops abruptly when he realizes he has actually been laughing and chatting amiably with this woman.)

IRMA

Will you join me in a glass of wine, Major? I saved it from my final meal. Please excuse the tin cups. I'm afraid they're worried I might cheat the hangman.

(He does not take the offered cup.)

If you will not drink with a murderess, will you at least drink with a young woman who is about to die?

PROSECUTOR

Was there much false testimony against you?

IRMA drinks from the cup that the PROSECUTOR had refused. During the next speech she calmly refills the cup and pours a second.)

IRMA

Most was mere confusion. The prisoners had trouble telling us warders apart. I imagine when you're slowly starving to death and someone is kicking you in the face, it's difficult to make an accurate identification. But what does it matter, Major? I'm guilty. It is not your fault that I left few alive to testify to my many crimes. Please, will you not drink with me?

PROSECUTOR *(accepting the cup)*

What's a proper toast in such a situation?

IRMA

L'chaim?

PROSECUTOR

God save the King.

124

IRMA

Whatever.

(They drink.)

Major, you seem to know everything about my life, but I know nothing of yours. Are you married?

PROSECUTOR

Yes.

IRMA

Children? . . . Would you prefer I not ask? Do you not want me to defile them by uttering their names on my sinful lips?

PROSECUTOR

No it's . . . one child. A girl.

IRMA

A girl? Do you have a photo?

PROSECUTOR *(checks pockets; relieved to find them empty)*

No, I don't seem to.

IRMA

It doesn't matter.

(She waves her arm. A picture of a woman and child appear.)

PROSECUTOR

Yes! That's my wife and daughter.

IRMA

What a lovely family. I believe she has your eyes. How long has it been since you've seen them?

PROSECUTOR

Nearly two years. How she's grown since then. My little baby. She played in her first recital last week. It seems only yesterday she was learning to play chopsticks. I used to love to listen to her in the evening at her lessons. She's so beautiful when she . . .

IRMA

Why do you always stop? Is it so horrible that you can actually talk freely with me? That you could possibly even enjoy my company?

PROSECUTOR

What happened to him?

IRMA

Mengele? I told you I don't know where he is.

PROSECUTOR

No, the other. The man you followed to Belsen. Your . . . your lover.

125

IRMA

Oh . . . I don't know. I *really* don't. He said we'd stay together forever. We were going to face the end side by side. But when the British tanks rolled in, he was gone. I couldn't find him. His name hasn't appeared on the arrest lists. Maybe he's safe somewhere. But what does it matter? He's lost to me now.

PROSECUTOR

I'm sor—

IRMA *(moving closer to him)*

I actually believe you are.

PROSECUTOR

This isn't right. You have done such inhuman things.

IRMA *(leaning seductively into him)*

Not inhuman. I assure you, I am quite human.

(They are once again under the mistletoe. IRMA takes the PROSECUTOR's arms and starts to draw him to her for a kiss.)

OLGA *(entering)*

What the hell do you think you're doing!

IRMA

Did you have to invite her?

OLGA

You can't actually feel sorry for her? She's a butcher! An animal!

IRMA

And yet, there is some pity in his heart for me.

OLGA

Pity? For you?

IRMA

It's only natural to pity one so young and SO beautiful who's about to die. It's so tragic.

OLGA

Oh, please. The role of tragic heroine hardly suits you.

IRMA

Oh, I rather fancy it. Well, I'm certainly not dying for my own sins. War Crime Trials! I spit on them. It was all just a grand circus to show how properly shocked the world was over what Germany had done. And to atone for the fact that they did not do one bloody thing to stop us.

OLGA

I seem to recall small war over the point.

126

IRMA

Germany started that. They had no choice. And it is for their shame I am being sacrificed.

PROSECUTOR

You're hardly an innocent lamb.

IRMA

Hardly. But that's not the issue. I'm not on trial here. You are.

(Lights rise up to reveal a judge's bench. MENGELE is seated behind it, wearing a judge's robe and wig. HELENE, dressed as the EXECUTIONER stands to his right. She wears a long, hooded black cape and black top-boots. The cape is tossed back over her shoulders, revealing a short skin-tight black leather skirt, a black corset and a swastika armband.)

MENGELE

All rise! Court is now in session. Read the charges.

EXECUTIONER

If it please the court, the accused stands charged with war crimes. Criminal negligence resulting in the deaths of eleven million men, women, and children.

PROSECUTOR

I don't understand. Why am I dreaming this?

IRMA

Because of your guilt. Your guilt haunts your dreams. Being a barrister—

MENGELE

—your nightmare takes the form of a trial. Complete with judge—

IRMA

—jury—

EXECUTIONER

—and executioner.

PROSECUTOR

Ridiculous. I have nothing to feel guilty about.

OLGA

True. But the guilt is still there. But that is good, Major. You cannot so easy sentence someone to die, even when justice cries out for it.

MENGELE

And that is your weakness.

OLGA

It is our strength.

(OLGA crosses to stand by side of PROSECUTOR.)

MENGELE

Do you speak in his defense?

OLGA

Yes.

MENGELE

Since the court is now assembled, let the prosecution present its case.

IRMA

Your honor, it is the position of the prosecution that the Allied nations conspired tacitly to aid Germany in its final solution to the Jewish problem. By their inaction they enabled the Reich to proceed with the exterminations and thus should share equally in their punishment. Not one nation intervened to prevent Germany from interring Jewish citizens. Oh, they did protest, quietly. But ultimately, they did nothing.

OLGA

And what could they do?

IRMA

They could have opened their doors to the poor wretches they accused us of abusing. Before the war, many Jews were free to emigrate. We did not want them. But neither did anyone else.

OLGA

I object to these charges of—

MENGELE

Overruled.

IRMA

When Jews tried to escape, the Allied nations slammed the doors in their faces. England, America, even Cuba, you sent them back to us. And we had told the world what we would do with them.

PROSECUTOR

We had no idea what they were being sent back to face.

OLGA

No sane nation could envision a place like Auschwitz.

MENGELE

Ah, but they knew.

IRMA

Churchill, Stalin, Roosevelt, they all knew.

PROSECUTOR

There were rumors, of course, early in the war.

IRMA

Was no credence put in these rumors?

PROSECUTOR

The sources were considered unreliable.

OLGA

Why?

PROSECUTOR

The information came to us primarily from Zionist groups, zealots. The rumors were put down to sensationalism.

IRMA

But proof came later, did it not?

PROSECUTOR

Eventually proofs of the wild stories started filtering out of Germany.

IRMA

And still you did nothing?

PROSECUTOR

Nothing could have been done! The camps were deep inside German territory.

IRMA

Oh, really? And where the hell was the R.A.F.? We waited for you. We expected the bombing raids. Olga, do you ever remember an air strike near the camp?

OLGA

No bombs fell on Auschwitz.

PROSECUTOR

It is most certainly not the policy of his Majesty's government to bomb prison camps.

IRMA

But railways were fair game. All it would have taken was one bomb. Just one strike on the rail station and you would have put us out of business. No more human fuel for the fires. But you never came. What were you waiting for, an engraved invitation?

PROSECUTOR

There were difficulties. Technical problems. Priorities had to be established—

OLGA

Technical problems?!

IRMA

I see. Perhaps these difficulties arose from your alliance with the Arab nations? Your treaty for Palestine?

PROSECUTOR

That has nothing to do with this. You're twisting things. I object to —

MENGELE

Overruled.

IRMA

And this is the government that so piously sat in judgment of me.

OLGA *(stunned)*

Difficulties . . .

PROSECUTOR

Olga, there was nothing to be done. We could not help you. You must know that. My God! You couldn't even help yourselves.

OLGA

What are you implying?

PROSECUTOR

It is just that there are many missed opportunities, courses of action we might have taken, but didn't. Maybe there were things we might have done differently. But we did finally destroy Hitler for you. We liberated you from the camps. What did you do?

OLGA

We did the dying. Wasn't that enough?

MENGELE

You could have fought. How different things might have been if every Jew had met us with a bullet instead of meek submission.

IRMA

If only you'd resisted.

OLGA

How dare you! How dare you accuse us. We were the victims. And even so, we fought! Your R.A.F. never touched Auschwitz. Only ones ever to strike camp were the prisoners themselves. Hard it was, risky to conspire against them. But we stole supplies, built a bomb, and we destroyed one of the crematoria. And they never rebuilt it. And many died for it. I risked my life to hide those explosives, and then to pass them to those who could do the most good with them. We did that little bit to stop the slaughter. What did you do? What did you risk?

IRMA

I seem to recall small war.

PROSECUTOR

It was most important to strike at the heart of Germany. At Hitler himself. We ended the war for you.

OLGA

Did you? How thoughtful of you. You arrogant, self-righteous pig. You congratulate yourself on decency, bravery to defend the helpless, while at same time smirking at our weakness.

PROSECUTOR

That's not what I meant. You must believe that.

IRMA

Who are you trying to convince, Major?

OLGA

How brave you all were. You who attacked the monster with guns, and tanks, and planes. So easy to be brave with a nation behind you and a full arsenal. We should have met them with bullets? What bullets?! We were thrown in the middle of hell with nothing but the clothes on our backs, and even these were stripped from us.

PROSECUTOR

I know, I understand—

OLGA

You have no idea what I'm talking. You think you know what bravery is? You think your soldiers were brave? When they fought most they risked was their lives. But when we fought, when we resisted, we risked not only our own lives, but lives of our families. Our children.

PROSECUTOR

Olga, please—

OLGA

But still we fought! In Warsaw, with our bare hands we fought and with what guns we could steal because the resistance wouldn't sell us any weapons. And at Sobibor. And anywhere we could without risking the lives of the innocent. You see, we could not always afford the luxury to die fighting. Not when we knew a hundred lives would be taken as a payment, as an example.

MENGELE *(banging gavel)*

Enough. This has been most illuminating. But would the defense care to present its case?

OLGA

How can I help him, when he can't even help himself?

(OLGA exits.)

MENGELE

In lieu of a defense, let us proceed to the execution.

PROSECUTOR

Wait! I petition the court for permission to present my own defense.

MENGELE

Petition denied.

PROSECUTOR

I move that the case be dismissed due to lack of counsel for the defense.

MENGELE

Motion denied. Does the accused wish to accept court-appointed counsel?

PROSECUTOR

What choice do I have?

MENGELE

None. Your counselor.

(DEFENSE enters carrying briefcase.)

PROSECUTOR

Oh, bloody hell, not him!

DEFENSE

I've reviewed the proceedings thus far. Up until this time the prosecution has been light with you. Since incidents of mass murder are well established, it would be best for your case if you admit to them under my questioning, before the prosecution has a chance to—

PROSECUTOR

I'm doomed.

DEFENSE

If you could please attend to the matter at hand. After all, it is your defense I am trying to prepare.

PROSECUTOR

Defense? In this kangaroo court? The outcome's already been decided.

DEFENSE

Naturally. For yourself there's nothing but the rope.

PROSECUTOR

For what? Mass murder? It's they who are the murderers, not us.

DEFENSE

You cannot deny the crimes. Millions of defenseless civilians slaughtered.

PROSECUTOR

That was them! They did it!

MENGELE

And what of Hamburg?

IRMA

Dresden.

EXECUTIONER

Berlin.

MENGELE

You condemn us for killing 2,000 an hour at Auschwitz, while at Hamburg 30,000 died in the span of a few hours—mostly women and children—from Allied bombs.

IRMA

And what of Dresden? Leveled, with all its people.

EXECUTIONER

Three-quarters of Berlin destroyed. 80,000 civilians dead.

MENGELE

And let us not forget our own allies. What of Hiroshima and Nagasaki?

DEFENSE

I object. These were clearly acts of war.

MENGELE

Overruled.

DEFENSE

I tried. Good luck, old man.

(DEFENSE exits.)

PROSECUTOR

But they *were* acts of war.

IRMA

Acts of war? Against unarmed civilians? Against undefended cities? The wanton destruction of non-military areas and their civilian populations is a violation of the laws and usages of war. This prosecution suggests that when innocent citizens are subjected to systematic destruction, deliberate and continual fire bombing of their homes, the taking of lives without trial, because they have committed no crime except that of being a German, is a clear violation of an unchallenged rule of warfare which outrages the general sentiment of humanity.

MENGELE

I'm satisfied. Proceed with the execution.

(EXECUTIONER produces a black silk cord and approaches the PROSECUTOR.)

PROSECUTOR *(points at EXECUTIONER)*

NO! Enough! I command you to vanish.

(EXECUTIONER continues toward him.)

Leave!

(MENGELE laughs. PROSECUTOR rounds on him in desperation.)

133

Bugger off!

MENGELE *(motions EXECUTIONER to halt)*
Does the prisoner wish to address the bench?

PROSECUTOR
You said all I had to do was order you gone and you'd disappear.

MENGELE
I lied.

PROSECUTOR
I will not stand accused of anything.

IRMA
You conspired to murder me.

PROSECUTOR
You were lawfully tried and sentenced. A sentence you justly deserved.

IRMA
Ja. I am guilty of your "crimes against humanity." And what sentence do you think proper for those who allowed me to do it?

EXECUTIONER
Death.

MENGELE
Death.

IRMA
Death!

PROSECUTOR
Who are you to accuse me?

IRMA
I am a member of the S.S., Germany's finest.

MENGELE
Hear, hear!

IRMA
I was proud to serve my country and wear the twin lightning bolts. There was a time when we were all ashamed to be German. We were forced to carry the entire guilt for the first war. Europe considered us barbarians . . .

EXECUTIONER
. . . war-mongers.

IRMA
Our parents walked bent with shame and taught us to be embarrassed of our heritage. The very heritage that gave the world its finest moments, its greatest artists!

MENGELE

Bach, a proud son of Germany, as was Beethoven . . .

EXECUTIONER

Brahms and Schiller . . .

MENGELE

Goethe.

IRMA

But the world remembered not the beauty . . .

EXECUTIONER

. . . but only the war that ravaged Europe . . .

MENGELE

. . . and destroyed Germany.

IRMA

But then, a man arose who remembered the glory that was Germany.

EXECUTIONER

Our leader.

MENGELE

Der Führer.

(A large photo of Hitler appears. A recording, Hitler addressing a crowd begins quietly under IRMA's next speech, continually growing in volume until the noise swells with the crowd responding "Zieg Heil!")

EXECUTIONER

Heil!

IRMA

And he had a dream that that greatness could be recaptured.

MENGELE

Heil!

(Montage: Hitler, crowds, swastikas, etc.)

IRMA *(raving fanatically now)*

No longer did we have to hang our heads in shame as our parents had done. No, I could shout to the world, proudly, Ich bin eine Deutscherin!

MENGELE & EXECUTIONER *(rising)*

Deutschland über alles.

MENGELE, EXECUTIONER & IRMA

Zieg, heil!

IRMA

Heil, Hitler! And when I heard him as a child, for the first time in my life I was proud of what I was, a German.

135

MENGELE & EXECUTIONER
Heil!

IRMA
And I knew then what our destiny was. We would rise to power once again, so that no one, ever, could force us to feel shame, make us feel as if we were beneath contempt, beneath the rest of mankind. We are not. We are a superior people.

MENGELE & EXECUTIONER
Heil!

IRMA
We are, indeed, the master race. And you will not keep us crushed beneath your heel. If there has to be a fourth Reich, and a fifth, and a sixth, whatever it takes, we will rise to the place we were destined to hold!

(The tape stops abruptly and the photos dissolve. MENGELE and the EXECUTIONER applaud IRMA's performance. Dropping the fanatic role like a mask, she curtsies, graciously accepting their applause. IRMA calmly crosses to the wine pitcher and pours herself and the PROSECUTOR another drink. EXECUTIONER stretches herself across the judge's bench. MENGELE turns his attentions to her.)

Is that better, Major? Does it make you feel more comfortable to hear me rave as a fanatic madwoman, instead of speaking as a young girl whose company could be pleasant?

PROSECUTOR
What are you? The fanatic or the innocent? The seductress or the soldier?

IRMA
I can be anything you want me to be.

MENGELE
Anything anyone wants her to be.

(MENGELE nibbles lightly on the EXECUTIONER's ear.)

IRMA
Joseph, what are you doing?

MENGELE
Isn't it obvious? I'm flirting with death.

IRMA
Please, spare us your wit.

PROSECUTOR
Stop it! All of you.

(EXECUTIONER exits, much to MENGELE's disappointment.)

MENGELE

Killjoy!

(He removes robe and wig and sits on bench.)

IRMA

Major, what do you want of me?

PROSECUTOR

Miss Grese—Irma . . . why?

IRMA

Do you mean, why Auschwitz? What I did there? That's it? That's your deep, burning question? You want to know what a nice girl like me was doing in a concentration camp like that?

MENGELE

Spare us, indeed!

IRMA

Hey, why not? Beats milking cows at the crack of dawn.

PROSECUTOR

I have got to make sense of this and you are not helping!

IRMA

My friend, you look for reasons in a very unreasonable world. Major, it's not possible for anyone to understand who didn't daily live with the stench of the ovens.

(His cold stare says that he won't accept that for an answer.)

Well, let us say that at the training camp at Ravensbrück I learned a great many things. They were very good teachers there. They could take anyone, ja, even a nice girl like me, and turn out obedient, zealous torturers of their fellow human beings. Anyone.

PROSECUTOR

I don't believe that.

IRMA

Oh, yes, you do.

MENGELE

And it scares the hell out of you.

PROSECUTOR

You can't blame this . . . this travesty on Ravensbrück.

(IRMA wanders to dressing table, reapplies lipstick.)

IRMA

Oh, but I don't. It is you who needs to assign blame. As for myself, I blame no one. Not Ravensbrück, not Hitler, not even circumstances. I chose my own path, even if I did not choose to recognize it for what it was. No, no one consciously chooses to be a murderer, a barbarian, a . . . filthy, bloody beast.

(She stares deeply into the mirror.)

Is that what I am, what you think I am? I don't think of myself that way.

(She puts the mirror aside, suddenly very weary.)

It's so strange. At the trial, that was the first time I heard we were murderers. At the camps we were engaged in special handling, the final solution, the glory of the Fatherland. We called it anything but its real name. And after a while you stopped thinking in terms of human life. But it was only in the courtroom we were murderers. At the camps I was simply disposing of verminous Jews that were a threat to Aryan supremacy . . . not people. I suppose I closed my eyes to what was happening around me, but there was no way to escape it. We guards were prisoners, too. We were never allowed to leave the camp. There were no furloughs, no weekend passes, no visits to town. Not for a moment could we get away from the acrid odors of the crematoria, the walking dead that wandered lifeless through the camp, the sounds and smell of death. At Auschwitz for over a year, I saw only two types of people. Those that killed, and those that were to be killed. And somehow it was I who was killing little children and old men and women—all the thousands and thousands of starving, dying women. I . . . murdered them.

PROSECUTOR *(moved in spite of himself)*

Is this sincere remorse, or just another role?

IRMA *(easily drops the haunted pretense.)*

Well, you didn't accept the fanatic routine. I thought this might be more to your tastes.

MENGELE

I was touched. Truly moved.

PROSECUTOR

You should have been an actress. You play many roles well. But which is the real Irma Grese? I just want for one moment to catch a glimpse of the one woman, the one real person who eluded us throughout the trials. It's not just because of you, it has to do with the camps: Auschwitz, Belsen, Dachau, this whole bleeding crime, the language can't even begin to describe it . . .

MENGELE

They seem to be calling it a holocaust.

PROSECUTOR

By whatever name you call it, it is so inconceivable that it ever could have happened at all. I've seen so much evidence of the horror and I still can't believe it.

(Pictures of the camps and the dead start fading in and out.)

I don't want to believe it. I can't get the images out of my mind. The horror! And of everything I've seen, the most terrifying enigma is you.

IRMA

Me? I'm flattered.

PROSECUTOR

You. Small, young, beautiful, murderous Irma Grese. The ultimate horror of this slaughter is that it was committed by you, and other children like you.

IRMA

I'm hardly a child.

PROSECUTOR

You were murdering in your teens. Just like the soldiers and the guards. Boys barely out of school. We fought a war against children. Adult madmen may have devised the extermination camps, but they were run by ordinary children.

MENGELE

What did you expect, horns and pitchforks?

PROSECUTOR

Irma, I want you to be some animal, some mindless beast. Anything but what you are. A beautiful young girl, standing before me, so vibrant and alive and so obviously human. No horns, no cloven hooves. My God, something of the horror should show in that face, there should be evil behind those eyes. But it's a face like any other. No different than any of my friends, my wife, my daughter—

IRMA

Like you?

PROSECUTOR

Yes. Like me.

(In the midst of the camp images appears a picture of the PROSECUTOR clothed in full S.S. uniform.)

And you're right . . . it scares the hell out of me. Damn it! Why can't you be something less than human? And so beautiful! Why did I have to find out that you've known joy, had dreams of greatness, that you're a woman who has loved and been loved . . .

IRMA

Loved and been loved?

(IRMA starts laughing.)

Sheisst, how stupid of me! Of course . . . "I don't want to know you're a woman who has loved and been loved."

(MENGELE and IRMA both laugh uncontrollably.)

Gott hilfen!

PROSECUTOR

Why are you laughing?

IRMA

I'm sorry, but it's so very funny. I didn't see it before, but we're kindred spirits.

MENGELE

Major, you should go now.

IRMA

You should never have come for absolution.

MENGELE

The blonde angel of Auschwitz gives none.

PROSECUTOR

Kindred spirits?

IRMA

Oh, ja.

MENGELE

You poor little man.

PROSECUTOR

Enough of the theatrics. I want some answers and I want them now. I need reasons.

IRMA

More wine?

(As she reaches for the pitcher, he takes firm hold of her wrist.)

PROSECUTOR

Irma, please. I want my reasonable, orderly little world back in one piece. It's not a game to me.

(She meets the pleading in his eyes and stops laughing. She gently removes his hand from hers and pours herself a cup of wine.)

IRMA

Very well, my friend. No more games.

(The projections fade. The cell bars disappear and MENGELE retreats from the scene as the lights dim everywhere except downstage center. Even the mistletoe is removed. If possible, all furniture except the bed should disappear as well. IRMA and the PROSECUTOR are left alone on a bare stage. IRMA's tale is told simply, without emotion or histrionics, as if telling a story from a great distance.)

You see, no more tricks. No more illusions. It's just you and me.

PROSECUTOR

And the truth?

IRMA

I'm out of practice, but I'll try. You'll have to excuse me, Major. It's unnerving to stand here stripped of all illusions . . . Let me tell you about my first. Don't raise your proper British eyebrows at me. I'm talking about murder, not sex. You always remember your first.

(She quickly drains her wine.)

She was a rather pretty thing. An Hungarian Jewess, I believe. It was at the station.

PROSECUTOR

This was at Auschwitz?

IRMA

Shhh. The truth is difficult enough for me, without interruptions. . . . Yes. The Auschwitz station. A shipment of 8,000. During selections, Mengele was called away, urgent business at the clinic. So a nod of the head, a click of the heels, and I was in charge. For the first time I was forced to raise my eyes from my ledger. Instead of ticking off numbers, I had to look at their faces. When I was still new to the S.S., I would wonder, "But where are all the Jews?" You know, the ones with low foreheads, hooked noses and long, dark locks. Those were the Jews we were taught to hate. But that image didn't hold true. Mostly, they looked like anyone else. Especially the one standing before me on the platform—my first. She was so lovely: fair, with long blonde hair that trailed down her back. She looked a little like my Helene, about her age at the time. Couldn't have been more than 17. I just stared at her as she waited meekly for me to point her in one direction or the other. I did not move. The guards became restless. I had one of the interpreters ask if her arm was broken, it was in a makeshift sling. And this piping, child-like voice answered "Yes." She stared at me with large innocent eyes waiting for me to give her life or death. The little bitch just stood there. I pointed her to the ambulance, the ones that drove straight to the gas chambers . . . After that, it was easy. If I would feel pity, I would think, "Why should this child, or this man, or this mother live when the other didn't?"

(She looks at him.)

You asked before how I slept at night. I sleep well, on the whole. But the nightmares, when they come, they're all about her.

PROSECUTOR

Just how does this make us kindred spirits?

IRMA

Because, Major, I am your first.

PROSECUTOR *(stunned)*

No. There's no comparison. You deserve to die. Your Jewess did not.

IRMA

By German law, she was condemned. Just as I am condemned by British law.

PROSECUTOR

There was no law involved. No trial, no due process—

IRMA

Her trial was on a railway platform. And I was prosecutor.

PROSECUTOR

Go to Hell!

IRMA

That's where you're sending me.

> *(PROSECUTOR opens his briefcase and collects his papers. IRMA flings them aside.)*

Before you go, look at me one last time. See the face that is going to haunt your dreams for the rest of your goddamn life.

PROSECUTOR

Don't flatter yourself. Irma Grese never existed except in the eyes of her audiences. Your life was just so many roles: competent soldier, loving sister, tantalizing mistress, and the ever popular efficient murderer. Parts to be played like some monstrous game.

IRMA

If that is what you choose to believe, then it's true.

PROSECUTOR

The game ends now! You are a criminal, and you have been justly tried and sentenced. You're not taking one last laugh to the grave. I'm walking out of your little melodrama.

> *(PROSECUTOR gathers up his briefcase, clutching it close to his breast as he crawls into the haven of his cot.)*

IRMA

Do you think you can so easily be rid of me? You pathetic little—

> *(Church bells ring. Terrified at the sound, IRMA rushes away, looking frantically offstage.)*

PROSECUTOR

What's that?

IRMA

The church bells . . . You should have taken a stronger sedative, Major. Even in your sleep you can still hear them.

(IRMA starts to run offstage, but is blocked by the entrance of the EXECUTIONER.)

EXECUTIONER

It's time.

(EXECUTIONER marches inexorably toward IRMA, to the slow accompaniment of military drums. She bears a black silk cord stretched taut between her hands. IRMA slowly backs away from her, her gaze transfixed on the EXECUTIONER as she continues speaking with the PROSECUTOR. She does not notice as DEFENSE, OLGA and MENGELE enter. DEFENSE is eating popcorn.)

PROSECUTOR

I'm going to awaken soon.

IRMA

I'm climbing the steps now. There are people everywhere. They've come for the show.

PROSECUTOR

I won't watch. Go away.

IRMA

At the top of the scaffold now. They tie my hands behind me. The rope cuts into my wrists.

PROSECUTOR

Can't you leave me in peace?

IRMA

I don't cry out. I don't want them to see me afraid. And I am so afraid.

PROSECUTOR

What the hell are you?

(EXECUTIONER has backed IRMA almost to the PROSECUTOR's cot. IRMA finally tears her gaze away from the approaching EXECUTIONER and locks eyes with the PROSECUTOR.)

IRMA

I'm Irma Grese.

(From behind IRMA, the EXECUTIONER snaps the cord around IRMA's neck. As she struggles for air, she drops to her knees and reaches out for PROSECUTOR. She dies inches from his face. The drums abruptly end with IRMA's death. Silently, EXECUTIONER removes her cape. She lays out IRMA's body and places her cape over the lifeless form, then kneels above her in silent prayer. The lights fade, leaving the PROSECUTOR in a small pool of light as he tries to hide beneath the covers of the cot. Before he can drift off into a more pleasant sleep,

IRMA's voice is heard, amplified throughout the theatre.)
Major! . . . Pleasant dreams.

(IRMA rises triumphantly and smiles at PROSECUTOR. The silence is suddenly broken by the boisterous applause of MENGELE and DEFENSE. They enter, DEFENSE carrying flowers. OLGA enters from opposite direction, more somber than the others.)

MENGELE

Brava, angel! Brava! Marvelous performance. Pity you can't take it on the road.

(MENGELE winks at PROSECUTOR. DEFENSE presents flowers to IRMA. The three congratulate each other. HELENE backs away from the gaiety toward OLGA, who keeps herself separate. Suddenly, the sound of an alarm clock is heard. The lights on the cot jump to full intensity as the PROSECUTOR awakes from his nightmare. The clock has also ended the celebrating. IRMA sits on the cot trying to reach the PROSECUTOR, but cannot.)

IRMA

Major . . . Major? . . . Major!!

(The PROSECUTOR has, by now, fully awakened and does not see the phantoms around him. By the time of IRMA's last cry, he has exited without a backward glance. The lights slowly fade to the sound of the slow, solitary applause of OLGA.)

CURTAIN

THE

IMMIGRANT

GARDEN

The third place winner is Caroline E. Wood, of Longview, Washington, for her exquisite one-act epistolary readers theatre script, *The Immigrant Garden*.

"I was born and spent the first ten years of my life in northern England," Ms Wood recalls. "I'm married, have two children and live in an old farmhouse on the Columbia River. I write, direct and produce plays for my little cafe located in a bookshop where I sell mostly used, but also some new books. I write plays with my cafe in mind and stage them in dinner theatre style for about thirty-five persons."

The Open Book's New York production of *The Immigrant Garden* opened October 6, 1994, at The Amsterdam Room with the following cast:

MISS CECILY BARNES . . . . Shannon Moffett
MRS. LOUISE BEAUCHAMP . . . . Beverly Fite
MRS. HELEN CURTIS . . . . Gisele Richardson

THE IMMIGRANT GARDEN

by Caroline E. Wood

Number 7 Fendmore Lane
Prince Edward Island U. S. A.
January 18, 1912

Dear Mrs. Beauchamp,

I am writing this letter in response to your advertisement I found in a quarterly called *The Reluctant Gardener*. My bookseller tells me it has been out of print for three years, the issue I purchased was published the 12th of January, 1908.

I do hope you are still selling seeds, as I am new to the world of mulch, bonemeal, cutworm, aphids and that shapeless drop of flesh, the slug, and could benefit from someone who is more familiar with these things than I. I am particularly interested in wallflowers. The seeds I purchased through a private company have failed me. A whole year of anxiously waiting and no blooms. Not a single one. And then, to make matters worse, my usual friends the sparrows scratched up my marigold seeds that took an entire afternoon to plant. I screamed at their feathered backs and threatened to take down their feeds. Do I sound too impatient to be a gardener? Do you have any hollyhock, foxglove, larkspur and dahlias? I would be interested in purchasing some. Mrs. Beecroft, who lives a mile up the road, told me that her grandmother had delphinium that grew twelve feet. I cannot imagine looking so high up at a flower. It sounds wonderful, though, and if you have some that can grow that high, can you send me them, please?

Yours very sincerely,
Miss Cecily Barnes

෴

White Cottage, York Lane, Bishop Berton
Yorkshire, England
15th February, 1912

Dear Miss Cecily Barnes,

You remind me of my little brook in late November when it is full and nearly overflowing. You are young, and either very beautiful or painfully plain for passion does not come from that place in between. Your letter has broken my solitude and for the slight ripple in my clear pool of stillness, I am grateful, for you ask nothing from me but my seeds, which I give freely. In my old age I am afraid I have turned quite eccentric and refuse to do anything that I do not want to. In fact, I often hold lengthy conversations with my flowers. Mind you, though, I would not have engaged in conversation if they had not started it first.

Well, all this is beside the point, the situation here is you need help with your garden. My child, I hope you have not dug up your wallflowers. I cannot imagine a seedsman selling you wallflowers without informing you they rarely bloom the first year. I am sending along some of my best delphinium seed. And your Mrs. Beecroft is quite correct, the stone wall surrounding my garden is well over twelve feet and the villagers walking down Crussix Lane often see the blue and purple tips of my delphinium swaying happily above the wall.

As for your feathered friends, I suggest laying some newspaper over your freshly planted seeds until they germinate and you see their pale green shoots appear, then take the paper off and after a couple of days in the sun the tender shoots will no longer tempt the sparrows's appetite. I am sending you a package of dahlia tubes, plant them in a sunny well drained spot and dispense plenty barnyard manure. Also find the following, and their instructions; hollyhock, larkspur, aster, hop, picotee pinks, sweet rocket and golden banner coreopsis and my prized sunflowers.

Sincerely,
Mrs. Louise Beauchamp

෯

Number 7 Fendmore Lane
Prince Edward Island U. S. A.
April 5, 1912

Dear Mrs. Louise Beauchamp,
When I received by post the parcel of seeds followed by your letter, I was thoroughly delighted. Your instructions written on each package left no room for question. You have thought of everything. I never expected so much, I am taken aback with delight. While holding between my fingers the delicate vessels of root, stem and blossom I am reminded by some whispering thought that my garden shall be the daughter of yours. I shall have an immigrant garden. Mrs. Beauchamp, I feel I must pay you coin for your seeds, it seems only proper that I do. Please tell me how much. Your lifestyle sounds very bohemian, living alone with no need of company or distraction, with not another soul to converse with and fend off the

doldrums. I, myself, well, you said I was young and I suppose nineteen is young but my father insists that it is quite old and that I should be married by now or at least engaged. But why should I marry when I find all men total and complete bores, and gamblers, I swear that is all I've seen. No, there is another type I find even more offensive, the intellectuals, young men who lift their noses high and quote Bacon or Lucretius, but always the same passages over and over until I imagine my lips are moving to form the words before their voices wallow up from their throats. And when I ask them for an original thought they look at me as though I have just enquired whether their undergarments were adjusted properly. "Why," they say, "all thought is original, Miss Barnes, whatever can you possibly mean?" It is then I confess to a dreadful headache and plead for their forgiveness while insisting the only remedy is a cup of chamomile tea and my own bed, where I shall agonize for hours before finally finding escape in a fitful sleep.

I must confess, I cause my father a fair amount of displeasure, but if he would quit bringing home students from the University to dine with us I would be kinder and I am certain he would be the happier for it. But you, Mrs. Beauchamp, I imagine full of grace and glowing countenance with eyes that see into the souls of men. And your garden moves across my mind as though it were a dream dreamt long ago and only remembered in fragments. And you have heard the voice of flowers. But, tell me, what sort of things do flowers say?

I almost forgot, I must ask you about a plant I discovered growing quite rapidly in my garden and seemingly without any root at all. It looks as though it is a mass of fine yellow hair all gathered up and twisted. It has a pale white flower and bears no leaves at all. When I found it bunched around my margaret pinks I worked the entire morning pulling the bothersome thing away.

Please write soon, your friend,
Cecily

ಙ

White Cottage, York Lane, Bishop Berton
Yorkshire, England
14th May, 1912

Dear Cecily,
Dodder! Oh, my dear, I pray I am wrong, but from your description I am afraid it could be nothing but dodder, one of the dreaded enemies of our precious flowers. If it *is* dodder, and I do so hope it is not, you will find what looks like fine yellow hairs about an inch or two growing in your

garden or somewhere close about. Pluck them out and leave no trace of root or blossom, for this deadly enemy is strong and bent on surviving and can thrive in any condition. It begins as a fine single thread, at first looking innocent enough, but then as soon as it can stretch and reach another plant it attaches itself and lifts its roots from the ground never to return, for this is a parasite that lives off the life of other plants, sucking the juice from them until they shrivel and die. The chaos dodder leaves in its wake is of no concern to it as it moves on constantly looking for more helpless victims in your garden. I see this wild plant growing in its natural state on high cliffs above the sea, looking quite pleasant mixed together with other wild things, but in a garden, make no mistake, it is total destruction. Be quick about it, Cecily, don't wait another minute!

What do my flowers say, you ask. I will do best to quote your Mr. Ralph Waldo Emerson. "Nature," he said, "is a language, and every new fact that we learn is a new word; but rightly seen, taken all together, it is not merely a language, but the language put together into a most significant and universal book. I wish to learn the language, not that I may learn a new set of nouns and verbs, but that I may read the great book which is written in that tongue." He wrote that in his journal in 1833 and I have just discovered its truth these past years. I suppose when I say talk, what I really mean is to communicate, to touch, to let something be known. One morning while weeding a bed of shirely poppies, my mind was perfectly clear and then like a sailing vessel appearing on the horizon a thought, quite plain, came to me, it said, "Do you understand that I cannot acknowledge your greatness until I confess my own?" Well, I must say, I looked over my shoulder to see who was there speaking to my back. So clear was the thought that I fancied I had heard it in voice. I went inside and wrote down the announcement, for that is what I felt it was. I often repeat it to myself and it seems I never tire of its wisdom and solace.

You asked if I thought you lacked the patience to be a gardener. It is not what you lack that is of concern, it is what you possess, and you possess a passion to grow flowers, and that is the purest form of ambition or love.

By the way, do you have toads in your garden? If not I suggest acquiring some, for the dear reptiles are lovers of noxious insects and are really pleasant fellows to have about. I purchase mine at Covent Garden Market in London for a shilling apiece.

You mentioned the cutworm. Lime turned into the soil is recommended, but truly the only certain way is to dig them up and be done with them. You will find them particularly around the roots of your plants. And about this mention of payment. I have no need of money and would feel uncomfortable accepting payment for something I do not, in its truest sense, own.

Yours Affectionately,
Mrs. Louise Beauchamp

&

Number 7 Fendmore Lane
Prince Edward Island U. S. A.
July 3, 1912

My Dear Mrs. Beauchamp,

Dodder it was and I am saddened to say it ravished my entire bed of asters and lavatera and all but one of my iceland poppies and even after all that, on the following Wednesday, I found my poor sunflower entirely covered with that horrid amber hair, all the way from its tall smooth stem to its beautiful face. My father called in his gardener and he insisted the only remedy was to cut down my sunflower and burn it as it would be the only way to be certain the weed was destroyed.

I did not let my father see my tears. I was not ashamed of them, but I did not expect him to understand, he so rarely does. I have pleaded to be excused from dinner tonight and have my evening meal brought to my room, as I know my father is expecting a dinner guest, one of those lofty intellectuals with sweaty palms and a crooked necktie, I'm certain. But he would not relent, and I am not happy about it. I dislike obeying my father's wishes when they are not my own, but unfortunately, equally so, I do so like to please him. Why must we be capable of so many opposing feelings? I find myself in the middle of what I am not certain, I am not entirely knowing but I can imagine that life would be far less tiresome if one were capable of only one vein of thought, one way of feeling, one way of seeing. It is really too exhausting, don't you agree? Oh dear, Mrs. Beauchamp, the dinner bell just rang, do feel sorry for me. Your sympathy will be my salvation.

Affectionately,
Cecily

&

White Cottage, York Lane, Bishop Berton
Yorkshire, England
15th August, 1912

My Dear Cecily,

You indeed have my sympathy, but you are young and therefore have

151

no need of it, for though unaware, you are brave and shall survive quite well. I am sorry about your sunflower, but your father's gardener is quite right and I pray this will be the end of this horrid weed. May I suggest you go beyond your own garden and scout it out? Find it, and if it is within a mile, destroy it, or I fear it shall remain a constant worry for you.

I am preparing for a short absence from England. My physician has ordered me to Italy for sunshine. He is a relentless old fool who no doubt is too old to be practicing medicine, but he is a friend and the only doctor I trust, so I must consent if I am to have any peace from the man. I shall miss my garden and can only hope all will be well while I am away. My housekeeper, Mrs. Curtis, promises to water and keep the weeds down. Although she is not a gardener herself, she is a loyal woman and can be trusted to do as she says. Did I tell you while gardening it is good sense to put a sprig of lavender beneath your bonnet? It is said to keep headaches away, I have practiced the habit for years and found its purpose quite useful. And if you are interested in making lavender water, here is my recipe:

23 ounces distilled water

2 ounces vodka

1 ounce dried lavender

I poured an entire bottle of it over my head last August when the sun seemed determined to scorch us to cinders over here. We are not used to such extreme heat in this part of England and I found it most uncomfortable. Lavender is a great favorite of mine, and I am not content with it growing only in my garden, so I pot it up and bring it in the cottage and put it on my windowsill. It is quite pleasing. Last evening past, the air was so still I could hear the water running in my little brook. I opened the windows and in minutes I was surrounded by the heady sweetness of my lavender. It is strange in a way, for the fragrance suggests to me another time, a world beyond time, perhaps, and for a moment I am there, in a place that seems so familiar, so known to me. But no sooner than the experience begins, it quickly fades, and I am left with an armful of nothingness and a sense of longing. Have you ever studied mysticism my dear? The Far East is full of it and I have been fortunate enough to have traveled there extensively in my younger days. I suppose that is where I might have picked up some of my queer ways, or as you might say, bohemian.

I am sending you one of my favorite books. It is Richard Jefferies's *Field and Hedgerow*. It is a signed copy and once belonged to my mother. I do hope you like it and can find a place in your heart for it.

May I now offer you some advice you might not be so willing to accept?

You say you wish there were but one way of seeing, one way of thinking and one way of feeling. But if that were so, how then could we know what we feel and think was truly our own? Sometimes it is only by being exposed to what we do not desire that we truly know what our desire is, it is only by holding the crystal up to the light and turning it in our fingers do we see its true structure. We are not unlike anything on this earth, we are full of different parts and complexities, that is our structure, this is our way. And as the crystal catches the light and reflects it, so do we with our own uniqueness create our own light. But now I have started philosophizing and that is something I do only with my flowers. Can I fancy you are one of them, or at least entertain myself with that thought?

Affectionately, your friend,

Louise

&

Number 7 Fendmore Lane
Prince Edward Island U. S. A.
September 29, 1912

Dear Louise,

I received your parcel and squealed with delight! The volume of Richard Jefferies is an absolute treasure. I have read some of his essays in school, but to hold his book that he himself once held and in which he penned his name is beyond explaining. Thank you from my heart, where this volume shall always be kept.

Dear Mrs. Beauchamp, you are wise to do as your doctor says. Enjoy Italy for a while, do send me a post card and when you return write me all about it. And do take a Baedeker! I hear Europe is just impossible without one. Must rush, Father is waiting for me and he does so dislike waiting. I shall write as soon as you send me your address.

Yours most affectionately,

Cecily

&

Thursday, December 30th

Dear Diary,

It has been three months and still not a letter from Mrs. Beauchamp. I fear for her health, but attempt to keep only good thoughts in my mind. The foxgloves and delphiniums were beautiful. I was so proud of them and showed them off every chance I got.

Mrs. Beauchamp, over and over again like waves rushing along an endless shore, I am reminded of your purest goodness. You have given me your garden and often I cannot contain my gratitude and find myself crying as I touch a delicate flower or tender shoot. More than anything the flowers are teaching me compassion. I cannot explain it, it just appears so.

I have met an exceedingly handsome young man whom I try the hardest not to flatter with my attention, although I must admit, it is only under the greatest restraint that I do not just plain stare at him. He dined with Father and me the evening my poor sunflower was thrown on the fire. We have dined many times since, attended the theatre and taken walks in the country. He is very nice and hasn't quoted Francis Bacon and doesn't even like Lucretius. I wonder when he will attempt to kiss me and if I shall let him.

I do wish the post would bring a letter from Mrs. Beauchamp.

⁎

White Cottage, York Lane, Bishop Berton
Yorkshire, England
10th January, 1913

Dear Miss Cecily Barnes,

I am most saddened to inform you that Mrs. Beauchamp has passed on. I am afraid she had been ill for quite some time. Dr. Pearson was with her in Italy and was seeing to her treatments. He found her in her room on the morning of the 14th of September. He said she was lying on a couch that sat beneath a large open window that was full of pots of lavender. Wouldn't that be like her, taking her lavender to Italy with her.

I shall stay on here until the house is sold and then travel south to my daughter's, where there is always a place for me. On Mrs. Beauchamp's desk I found a letter addressed to you, so I am sending it on.

Respectfully,
Mrs. Helen Curtis

⁎

White Cottage, York Lane, Bishop Berton
Yorkshire, England
1st September, 1912

My Dearest Cecily,

Do you hear it? It is the flowers in the garden. Listen, there it is. "What do they say?" you asked me once. They go beyond saying, they go beyond language, for flowers speak the music of the soul and for that there are no words . . . and you have heard their whispers before, perhaps when very young, when days drifted into one another like faint afternoon dreams, but you have not forgotten, you have only stopped remembering. For once you have hear them you are changed, there is no going back, it is just the way, there is no explaining it.

But it is late now and I am growing tired. There is a full moon tonight without a cloud in the sky and I can hear my brook running down its stony path. It is not a very big brook, but it thinks it is, and I have never told it anything different.

Oh, Cecily, this is not goodbye, it is only the passing of one season into the next, and all seasons are necessary for growth. We would not expect to find leaves on our ash trees in December or crocuses in August. No, all the seasons have their purpose, and all is as it should be. Take care, my child, and if we are both willing, we shall meet one sweet scented summer afternoon in our immigrant garden.

Always Affectionately,

Louise

QUIET!

THREE LADIES LAUGHING

Fourth place winner, Robert Hawkins, is a native of Alabama. "I began writing as a cub reporter for the same City News Bureau of Chicago that produced Ben Hecht and Charles MacArthur's *The Front Page*. Later, I worked for the Chicago Tribune, but during midlife crisis, became a reporter for the Northern Territory News in Darwin, Australia, before settling into a twenty-plus-year career as an IBM writer/editor." Now retired, he lives in St. Augustine, Florida, where he is an assistant professor of communications at Flagler College.

Comedy and poignant drama distinguish Mr. Hawkins's first play. "If my characters seem true to life," he says, "it's because they are taken in bits and pieces from some very marvelous people no longer with us."

Quiet! Three Ladies Laughing was first presented by Stage II at the Powerhouse Performing Arts Center of New Canaan, Connecticut, on January 22, 1993, with the following cast: Kimberley Lowden (Ada), Barbara Halas (Eva), Maryjane Lauria (Lottie), Shannon Davis (Diedre), Nadya Sheehan (Edna), Robert Doran (Earle) and Gina Wynn (Lou Berta).

The Open Book's New York readers theatre production of *Quiet! Three Ladies Laughing* in its present revised version opened January 12, 1995, at The Amsterdam Room with the following cast:

NARRATOR/LOU BERTA/DIEDRE	Laura E. Johnston
ADA LOU (Lucile Nolan) MORGAN	Kathryn Carrol
EVA (Nolan) BRADFORD	Tiffany Marshall
LOTTIE (Nolan) KOKASKA	Susan Peahl
AUNT EDNA	Beverly Fite
EARLE	Wayne Markover

QUIET! THREE LADIES LAUGHING

by Robert Hawkins

ACT ONE

SCENE ONE

A sleeping porch at the Nolan homeplace in north Alabama during 1943. The porch is screened from floor to ceiling. Lattice shutters provide privacy. Two brass beds with a rattan table in between dominate the set. A large radio and wilted pitcher of tea sit on a smaller table at STAGE LEFT. A small armoire is at STAGE RIGHT, along with a wicker chair and floor lamp. A small rotating fan sits on the floor at STAGE CENTER aimed at the beds. Clothes are slung over the back of the chair and a suitcase with clothes spilling out sits near the fan. It's early afternoon and the sun is blazing through the shutters. As the curtain rises, ADA LOU sleeps fitfully on the bed STAGE LEFT in her slip as LOU BERTA enters. She surveys the scene, shaking her head in disbelief and then slowly goes about straighten things.

LOU BERTA

Lawd . . . lawd. Grown ladies and they still can't pick up after themselves. Ummmmmmm-hmmmm. Mercy. Now why would they want to stay out here on this ole porch when their rooms are all made up? I swan-e-e.

(Shaking her head in disbelief)

Sometimes I wonder about them girls . . .

(LOU BERTA, mumbling to herself, walks softly around the room, trying not to wake ADA LOU. She looks down at her and smiles and then walks UPSTAGE, humming softly while she straightens the room.)

Miss Ada Lou's been up all night looking after her Mama . . . po' thang. She can't seem to let down and get some rest. I want her to hold up when the time comes, cause she's gonna need to. Now Miss Eva . . . she thinks she's the one suffering the most, but she could handle the devil hisself if she had to . . .

(Gives a little laugh)

She sho' could. And Miss Lottie . . . well, don't need to worry 'bout Miss Lottie. No siree . . . but I think that things just ain't right up there in Chicago like she puts on. I know that child. I brought her into this world. She ain't saying some'em. But I know when some'em wr-o-n-g.

(ADA LOU wakes up with a start and half sits up in bed.)

159

ADA LOU

What? Oh . . . oh, Lou Berta.

(Sinks back exhausted)

Is Mama all right?

LOU BERTA

Yes, child . . . she's doing as good as can be expected. Miss Eva and Miss Lottie are in there with her, so you go on and get yo' rest. You done been up half the night . . .

(ADA LOU sinks back on the bed and lets out a sigh.)

ADA LOU

Oh . . . I am tired. Wake me if you need me . . .

(ADA LOU turns over and tries to sleep as LOU BERTA keeps straightening things and somewhat talking to herself, ADA LOU and the audience.)

LOU BERTA

Been a long time since these girls been home. A long time. And it ain't a happy time for them to be here, not with their Mama lying up there in the front bedroom in misery. Oh, I wish the lawd would just take Miss Lula on. Just take her! She done suffered enough, but I ain't got no right to tell HIM what to do. But I wish he'd send a band of angels down to carry her off . . . and me too, when my time comes. *(Sadly)* But I know that ain't gonna happen . . . *(Shaking her head)* Naw, that ain't gonna happen.

(She continues to clean and straighten up. She stops and puts her hand on the rocking chair.)

Use to rock Mr. Earle in this chair when he was a tiny baby. Lawd, I'm afraid the Army ain't gonna let him get home 'fore Miss Lula passes on. I don't get no good feeling about him, either! My head gets all swimmy thinking about it. Trouble . . . somehow we all got to get through this trouble, 'cause it just keeps coming on . . . and don't leave nobody alone.

(Enter EVA, a very attractive woman in her early forties, wearing a slip with a light silk robe in a bright floral pattern loosely on her shoulders. Her hair is tied up in a scarf and she appears exhausted.)

EVA

Oh! This heat! . . . Mercy! . . . I don't think I can stand it any more! What's got into me?

(She heads towards the fan and kneels down in front, pulling her bra wide to cool off, then sighs.)

Oh-h-h . . . that feels good! I just don't ever remember it ever being this hot!

(ADA LOU wakes with a start. She flops over, trying to go back to sleep, but gets up and stares at EVA hogging all the fan. ADA LOU

160

gets off the bed slowly and goes over to the suitcase and begins rummaging around.)

ADA LOU

I'm sure it's over 100 degrees already. But it's August. And you know, September can be worse.

(Finding a hairbrush, she strokes her hair, then reflects.)
Remember how hot it seemed when we started school right in the middle of August? How did we ever stand it after going barefoot all summer and wearing nothing but shorts and little or nothing in the house? I remember it was sheer torture just to put on a dress.

(With her eyes closed, EVA rocks back and forth on her heels.)

EVA

I know . . . but we were more used to it then. Lord knows, the older I get, the less heat I can take. Phew! At least it's not this hot in Mobile. Thank heaven we at least get a breeze off the bay now and then.

(She gets up slowly and then focuses on LOU BERTA.)
Lou Berta . . . Lottie's looking for you. She has a little errand she wants you to do. Personally, I wouldn't do it, if I were you.

LOU BERTA

What kind of errand? I gotta start fixing supper.

EVA

Go see . . . she's in with Mama.

LOU BERTA

Miss Lottie's always stirring up something every time she comes.

(She exits, mumbling to herself.)
I can't do all this running around any more. No, m'am, can't do it no more . . . ummmmm-hmmmm . . . .

(EVA grabs a fan and fans herself furiously and then walks over to peek through the shutters.)

EVA

God! There's not a leaf stirring out there . . . not even a whiff of a breeze . . . and not a soul on the street, either. Not even Aunt Edna!

(Brushing her hair in short, slow strokes, ADA LOU turns to EVA.)

ADA LOU *(softly)*

How's Mama?

(Letting out a sigh, EVA slumps down again on the floor in front of the fan, arms akimbo, with a sense of total surrender.)

EVA

Just the same . . .

(She leans up on an elbow.)

She must be suffering something awful in this heat . . . but she hasn't even let out a peep. Not one peep!

(Pulls a hankie from her kimono and blows her nose)

Maybe this air conditioning thing Lottie's doing will help a bit . . . .

ADA LOU

Air conditioning?

EVA

Yeah . . . Lottie's strung up all these wet sheets in Mama's room.

ADA LOU *(a bit confused)*

What on earth for?

EVA *(with a muffled laugh)*

She's air conditioning Mama's room! Just like Kresses! Now isn't that something? Probably some crazy thing she learned up there in Chicago! I swan-ee, leave it to Lottie!

(Gets up and joins ADA LOU on the other side of the bed.)

She wants poor ole Lou Berta to go up to the church and pick up whatever electric fans she can find . . . She says they won't need them till Sunday, anyway. Lord . . . I'd be surprised if Lou Berta can even drag one back, old as she is . . . and in this heat!

ADA LOU

Eva . . . I don't understand what you're talking about.

EVA *(giggling)*

Lottie says that when the fans blow on the cold sheets, it'll cool the air and make it feel like air conditioning! Now isn't that smart? Isn't that just like her? *(Reflecting for a moment)* Papa always said she had the brains in the family. He certainly didn't credit me with any!

(Reaching into her kimono, EVA turns away from ADA LOU and pulls out a package of cigarettes and matches.)

Lottie was always Papa's favorite, too . . . and Mama's, for that matter . . .

ADA LOU

Oh, Eva . . . don't start bringing all that up . . . if the truth be known, I think Mama always cared more about you than any of us . . . well, maybe except for Earle . . . especially now that he's away in the Army. But of the girls, well . . .

EVA

Why, Ada Lou, where on earth did you ever come up with that? Sure . . . Earle is her baby, but ME! She loves ME the best . . . shoot!

ADA LOU *(almost spitefully)*

I just know . . . that's all. When I've been here by myself, all Mama talks about is you being way off in Mobile and Lottie off in Chicago and how neither of you never get to come home . . . I know she wishes you lived as close as I do in Birmingham, but all she talks about is how she misses you . . .

EVA (pleased)

Why, Ada Lou, I didn't know that! Of course, Mama never came right out and said how she feels about my not getting here often and it is a real chore. Then after I get up here, all I hear is "Ada Lou this . . . and Ada Lou that . . . " And if you want to know the truth, I sometimes wonder why I make all that effort to come, when I know it isn't appreciated.

ADA LOU

Why, Eva . . . that's not so!

EVA

And now . . . especially now with the war on . . . and gas rationing . . . Did you know Morris now has to travel the whole coast from Mobile to Port Arthur, Texas . . . and they haven't even increased his gas allowance! We don't have any extra stamps to ride around town any more . . . much less come way up here. Why, Morris sometimes has to stay over in New Orleans to save on those darn gas coupons . . .

(She hesitates and a worried look appears on her face.)

He's away so much now . . . *(Reflecting)* . . . ever since Mardi Gras . . . he spends more time now in New Orleans . . .

ADA LOU

Eva . . . I know what I'm talking about, since I'm the one who's here all the time . . . *(Under her breath)* . . . the one who can just drop everything and come on a moment's notice . . . and what do I hear? *(In a mimicking manner)* "Eva this and Eva that . . . "

(She gets up from the bed and drops the brush into the open suitcase.)

What little time you do have with Mama seems to be more appreciated than my popping in all the time!

EVA (secretly pleased)

You never told me that . . . did Mama really say that? What else did she tell you?

(EVA automatically lights her cigarette.)

ADA LOU (shocked)

Eva! You're . . . smoking!

EVA (shrugs it off)

It's my nerves . . . they're acting up . . .

ADA LOU

You haven't smoked for years . . . What is going on?

(EVA parades back and forth mockingly.)

163

EVA

I sneak a smoke now and then. I know it's almost a sin to smoke in Mama's house . . . but I do it, anyway . . . every time I come. Nobody knows . . . well, Lou Berta might, but Mama never knew and she won't know NOW unless I burn the house down!

(She looks for some place to flick the ashes and then uses a nearby cold cream jar lid.)

ADA LOU *(suspicious)*

Eva . . . this isn't like you . . . is something going on? . . . between you and Morris?

EVA *(caught off guard)*

Why, no . . . nothing of the sort. I . . . I'm just upset about a lot of things. Mama . . . well, maybe Morris . . . I don't know . . . I just need something to calm me down now and then. Maybe some of that "nerve medicine" that Doc Strawbridge whips up in the back of his drug store. Half the town has been taking it for years! And they're CALM!

ADA LOU

Stop talking like that.

EVA

Well, it's true . . . and you know it. Everybody's either on that nerve medicine . . . or swigging that ole vanilla extract from Mr. Griffen's store . . . or they're on moonshine . . . or God knows what! *(Giggles)* I just thought of something! What was the name of that teacher . . . Mr. Ott? Was it Ott? Poor ole thing . . . used to come to school on Monday morning with his lips and tongue all blue from drinking ink strained through bread to get the alcohol! Oh, he must have been desperate. Isn't that pitiful? I wonder whatever happened to him?

ADA LOU

Lord only knows . . . but stop talking about taking something to calm you down. Somebody might hear you.

EVA

Somebody like Aunt Edna? Shoot! I was half expecting her to be over here by now checking us out . . . especially with Lottie arriving on that late train last night. *(Begins to pace a bit)* Ada Lou, I've been upset so, lately, you know, with Mama and everything. I get nervous a lot, and yes, I smoke a bit more than I ever did. But it doesn't have the same connotation that it did when Aunt Edna started all that ruckus about me smoking at the sorority over at the university. It's not the same thing now. Why, women smoke right out in public . . . or at least they do in Mobile. And in the best restaurants, too! And you know what, if Aunt Edna were to come in right now, I would walk right over and blow smoke right in her face!

ADA LOU

You'll do nothing of the sort!

EVA

Oh, yes I would, too. I never have forgiven her for getting Papa all riled up. You remember that, don't you? Oh-o-o . . . I will never forgive her for that.

ADA LOU

That was a long time ago . . . why don't you . . .

EVA

No, I can't forget . . . or forgive! What makes me mad is that Papa believed every word she said, instead of what I had to say. He just drove right over there to Tuscaloosa and jerked me right out of the university that day! I was just livid!

ADA LOU

Eva . . . don't get yourself excited all over again . . .

EVA *(talking to herself)*

I wasn't carrying on and acting like the campus hussy! I wasn't doing anything that the other Kappa Delta's weren't doing, for heaven's sake! *(Stamps out cigarette)* And you know what, it was that fat-faced daughter of hers . . . that Frances Evelyn . . . she got that story going.

(She raises her hand to hush ADA LOU.)

I know that for a fact! Oh . . . she's so mean! Just plain mean! Always was! And all because she didn't get a bid from Kappa Delta! *(Paces)* I couldn't do anything about that. She was such a pill. I never liked her, anyway . . . I only had her over for Rush Week because Mama insisted. But she was blackballed . . . *(Pauses to think)* And yes, I cast one of those three black balls myself!

ADA LOU

Why, Eva! I didn't know that!

EVA *(continues pacing)*

I never told anybody. Oh . . . how could Papa believe all that mess . . . and Mama, too! But Papa caught me smoking in Morris's car, and then he believed it all! Oh, I get livid when I think of it! I don't think Papa ever forgave me . . . nor Mama, for that matter.

ADA LOU

Oh, she did, too. She didn't believe Aunt Edna. And I know she was just as sorry as you were that Papa acted so hastily. I remember that much . . . but I guess to keep peace in the family she didn't—

EVA

Well, shoot! What's so bad about smoking? It won't kill ya. Everybody smokes now. You don't have to hide it now. And since this has turned into some sort of confession period, I'll admit it. I did have a drink . . . or two . . . with Morris over at ATO House once. Everybody did it then, for heaven's sake. What were fraternities for, if you couldn't go drink? But that's all we did. And there certainly wasn't any hanky-panky going on with me and Morris, either. No sir-ee! Somehow, though, I wish something had been going on. It might have made a big difference. *(Sits on bed)* Maybe Morris and I wouldn't have jumped into a marriage right away . . . oh, I don't know anything any more! *(Reflects)* Did you know that Mama thought I was pregnant before Morris and I got married?

ADA LOU
No-o-o! She didn't think that at all.

EVA
Well, she did, too . . . and Aunt Edna was the one who spread that story around town . . . and that's what started it all . . . OH! I could just scream! Now that's where Mama could have come to my defense! But she didn't! She took her sister's side instead of mine! Her own daughter! Oh! I could strangle Aunt Edna! Even now!

ADA LOU *(putting her arm around EVA)*
Hush, now. Just calm down . . . that was a long time ago. Everybody's forgotten those old stories.

EVA
Well, I haven't! And I can't calm down at this point. I'm too riled up! I get that way every time I come back home. That's why I dread coming here, because I have too many bad memories and old hurts that just jump out of the closet at you once you're here. Like yesterday . . . it just came to me . . . out of nowhere . . . that Mama actually "pushed me" into marrying Morris . . . just in case I was pregnant! Cause she believed Aunt Edna's story.

ADA LOU
You're talking nonsense now . . .

EVA
No, I'm not. Mama didn't believe me! Didn't believe me at all! And God knows, I didn't have Alice until two years after we were married! Wasn't that proof enough? I wouldn't put it past Aunt Edna to spread another rumor that I had an abortion . . . just to prove she was right the first time.

(She rips out another cigarette.)

ADA LOU
That's all past history now and you know there was no such talk going around. *(Calmly)* No scandal. Mama just wanted you to get on with your life, that's all. She really didn't want you to be a teacher and move off to God knows where. She wanted you nearby . . . with babies and . . .

(EVA takes a long drag on her cigarette and looks unconvinced. She

lays back on the bed, staring at the ceiling.)

EVA

Ada Lou, I think the one thing I want most in this world is to hear Mama tell me directly that she never believed I was pregnant . . . even if it's her dying breath. I want to hear it . . . from her lips.

(ADA LOU starts to say something. but is hushed.)

I know . . . I know. But you know . . . sometimes you just gotta hear it. That's the only way. You could write it down, but that doesn't do anything. Not for me. I want to hear her say it to me directly . . . not second hand.

ADA LOU

Eva . . . stop torturing yourself like that. Believe me, hon, it was just me and Earle living here then with you over at the university . . . Lottie was off working up there in Chicago in that settlement house . . . and no one ever insinuated that you were pregnant . . . no one. Now believe me. And don't get some notion that you're going to try to get some deathbed confession out of Mama. She probably doesn't remember a thing about it now, anyway. So just get that out of your mind.

(EVA begins to cry, then snuggles up to ADA LOU.)

EVA *(softly)*

I know . . . I know . . . I just haven't talked about it to anyone in all these years. I just hold it in . . . and then I get back here and it all starts up again. I wish I could have talked it over in a more rational manner with Papa, but he just upped and died on us without any warning! *(Pauses)* Well, he was so hard-headed I don't think I could have made him believe me, anyway. But Lottie could have—

(LOTTIE enters, looking exhausted. She wears a plain house dress and her hair in a snood.)

LOTTIE

Lottie could have what?

EVA *(sits up and hides cigarette)*

Changed Papa's mind . . . you always had him around your little finger.

(LOTTIE shrugs it off. Her mind is on other things as she sits in the wicker chair and kicks off her shoes.)

LOTTIE

Lou Berta's back with the fan. I think it's going to work . . . it's much cooler in Mama's room now that it is in here . . . Whew! This heat . . . uhhhh! I forgot how bad it could get. Would one of you go sit with Mama? I think that long trip from Chicago is beginning to catch up with me. *(She sits up and sniffs the air.)* Is something burning? Did Lou Berta leave something on the stove?

167

(EVA jumps up, hiding ashtray behind her back.)

EVA
I'll go look in on Mama . . .

LOTTIE *(slyly)*
Eva . . . would you please put out that cigarette before you go in Mama's room? I didn't know you still smoked.

EVA *(embarrassed)*
Oh, I don't really. Just occasionally . . . when I get nervous or tired. I'll . . . I'll see to Mama . . .

(She hurriedly exits.)

ADA LOU *(shaking head)*
That Eva! She's something, isn't she? Lottie . . . you must be really tired. Did you manage to get a seat? I hear that nearly everybody has to stand up between here and Birmingham . . . all these servicemen are taking all the seats.

LOTTIE *(yawning)*
I managed to get a seat as far as Memphis. I was lucky . . . this soldier got up and gave me his seat . . . he was just a boy! I told him to just sit on my suitcase . . . but by the time we got to Memphis, I had to get out of that car. There was no air circulating, no air at all, and I felt I was going to be sick. So I stood out in the vestibule between cars the rest of the way. It was much cooler doing that.

ADA LOU *(hesitantly)*
Was Karl upset about you coming back so soon?

(LOTTIE gives a little grunt meaning "somewhat." She goes to the bed and stretches out next to ADA LOU.)

I started not to call you, but then I knew you would never forgive me if I didn't. Dr. Sizemore kept telling me that Mama could go any time now, so I went ahead and called.

LOTTIE *(resigned)*
You did the right thing. There was nothing else you could do. I had to be here. Oh, Karl did put up a fuss, mainly because I was just down here in April, but I don't think that was the reason. Both Stephen and Karl Jr. are away at camp . . . so it's not that he has to care for them. It's just that he doesn't want to have to fend for himself . . . especially since he doesn't have his Mama around to do it for him. It's this male pride thing . . . *(Frustrated)* He can't . . . I mean he won't even wash a dish!

(She lays back, exhausted.)

Oh, that woman . . . dear Mama Kokaska! She never let me have a moment's peace . . . always complaining that I wasn't looking after Karl . . . not fixing him the right food . . . not keeping the house clean . . . not raising my children as good Catholics! Oh, God forgive me, but I'm not sorry that woman's gone on to glory or wherever!

ADA LOU

Why, Lottie! You shouldn't say such things!

LOTTIE

I can't help it. That woman never liked me from the start and she was beginning to turn Karl against me . . . but . . .

(EVA sticks her head in the door, giggling loudly.)

EVA

Ada Lou! You gotta come see this! If I closed my eyes I would have thought I was in Woolworth's! It's downright cold in there!

ADA LOU

Really? I'll be there in just a minute.

(EVA disappears.)

Lottie, get some rest. I'll go tend to Mama . . . and see what all this shouting is about. You rest, you hear?

LOTTIE

I will. I'll take a little cat nap, but call me if you need me.

(ADA LOU exits. LOTTIE gets up from the bed and walks over to the shutters and looks out. She lifts her dress to reveal bruises and welts on her back between her bra and half-slip. She rubs them gently and then climbs exhausted into bed.)

ACT ONE

SCENE TWO

(A short while later on the sleeping porch. ADA LOU is on the bed stage left, EVA on the bed at stage right while LOTTIE lounges in the chair. A roar of laughter is heard as the scene begins.)

EVA

Oh, Ada Lou, you probably were too young at the time to remember, but Lottie broke the new dresser mirror Papa had just got from Memphis . . .

LOTTIE

Eva . . . you know YOU broke it!

EVA *(loud howl)*

Why . . . I did not!

LOTTIE *(jokingly, laughing)*

You did, too. I remember now. You were trying to drape that old Spanish

169

shawl I brought back from Santa Fe over the top of the mirror . . . said you saw a picture of it done in some fancy Riverside Drive apartment in New York and you wanted to dress up Mama's boudoir . . . and Mama didn't want it!

(Both scream, ADA LOU trying to go along, but can't find it that funny. It's a joke between the older sisters.)

EVA *(still rolling in laughter)*
Remember . . . remember how she pinched me and called me "a little goose!"

(Goes over to LOTTIE and begins pinching her like their mother did, muttering.)

You little go-o-o-se!

(Both scream in laughter and a child's voice is heard at the door.)

DIEDRE
Mama . . . can I come in? What are ya'll doing?

(She doesn't wait for an answer and steps inside.)

ADA LOU
Dee, honey, you know this room is for grown ladies only. Now what do you want?

DIEDRE
Why are y'all laughing?

ADA LOU
We're just talking about old times, honey. Now you run along and play outside and be quiet.

DIEDRE
Can I have supper over at Jimmie Ann's house . . . and spend the night? Can I, please?

ADA LOU
Dee, I don't know if Frances Evelyn wants any company over there tonight. Why don't you just have something back in the kitchen . . .

DIEDRE
But Jimmie Ann's already asked me! And she says her Mama wants me to spend the night, too. Can I, please? Please?

(ADA LOU looks to the others for approval.)

LOTTIE
Oh, Ada Lou, let her visit with her cousin.

ADA LOU
Every time we're down here, Dee just lives over there. And Frances Evelyn never liked having a lot of children around. Oh, Dee, why don't you just stay here . . .

170

DIEDRE *(loudly)*

Oh, please, can I go? I want to so bad.

ADA LOU *(jumps off bed)*

SH-H-H-H, Dee! Don't make so much noise! You know your Mam-Ma is real sick. No shouting, you hear? No running up and down the hall making a racket. You and Jimmie Ann have got to be quiet!

DIEDRE

But y'all make more noise than we do!

> *(EVA and LOTTIE stifle their laughs as ADA LOU winces and feels embarrassed at DIEDRE's outburst. She takes DIEDRE by the hand and leads her into the hallway. Muffled sounds of scolding are heard.)*

EVA

She's right, you know! Oh, that Dee is a sweet child . . .

> *(She lights a cigarette unconcerned. A very sad look crosses her face.)*

She's just about Alice's age when she . . . drowned.

> *(She paces the floor, holding back tears.)*

Oh, Lottie, sometimes I just can't bear to think about it, and I try not to. But sometimes something sets it off . . . like Dee wanting to go over to Jimmie Ann's . . . and it all comes rushing back.

LOTTIE

Eva, get some rest. You're tired. You and Ada Lou have been here looking after Mama and I know you're exhausted. Let me take over. Get some rest.

> *(EVA ambles over to shutters, peeks out.)*

EVA

Alice wanted one more swim . . . one more dive off the rock and I said, "No . . . we're gonna eat soon and you've been in the water all day." She was just like a little tadpole, you know.

LOTTIE

Eva, please. Go lie down in the front bedroom and take a little nap.

EVA

But she didn't listen . . . *(small laugh)* . . . she was just like me! Just a wild thing. I should have known she would slip out of her room and go back down there. She had to have her way, oh, yes. She had a mind of her own, even at that age.

LOTTIE

Eva, stop torturing yourself. There's nothing you can do. Oh, I know, I know, I'd be the same way if something happened to my boys. You can't but worry when they're away at camp. You don't know really for sure about their supervision. But you can't worry about every little thing with children.

EVA

Morris has never really gotten over it . . . he really hasn't. You know, I sometimes think he blames me for her running down there to the dock in the dark . . . like . . . (*getting a bit hysterical*) . . . like I should've locked her in her room or something . . . I mean . . . oh, God help us! I can still see her down there in the water . . .

> *(LOTTIE jumps up and puts her arms around her, comforting her and leads her back to the bed, taking her cigarette from her.)*

LOTTIE

Oh, Eva, don't get yourself all worked up. We've got a rough time ahead with Mama. Try not to think about Alice now, will you?

EVA *(more sober)*

I'll try, but it seems like when I'm worn out and troubled about a lot of things, I start thinking about Alice and I . . . I guess I just go crazy, especially in the heat like today. (*More back to normal*) Oh, it's so hot! Why does it have to be so hot! We could sure use some more fans around here.

LOTTIE *(hesitant)*

I'm a bit concerned about Ada Lou. Oh, she's taking everything in stride, but you know how she hides her feelings. I just hope she holds up when Mama finally does let go.

EVA *(more relaxed)*

Don't worry too much about her. She's got the strength of an elephant. I know it like to kill her when they drafted Hershal in the Army, but they do need doctors, too. She's handled that well, but I'd be beside myself. She's a real saint.

LOTTIE

I know . . . and I feel guilty about dropping everything and running down here whenever Mama needs her. I couldn't do that. Neither could you.

EVA

That's for sure. Don't know who she takes after in this family. It's like she and Earle are from another tribe . . . a whole different family. Can you believe we have an 18-year-old brother serving in the Army! Can you?

LOTTIE

It does seem strange, doesn't it? But then I was practically grown and gone most of the time when both of them came along.

EVA

Well, I wasn't! And I remember how I resented Mama (*Animated*) cuddling Ada Lou all the time. She never did that to me . . . and I wanted her to so badly. Nobody knew how insecure I was . . . and scared.

LOTTIE

Why, Eva, Mama held you every moment of the day because you screamed bloody murder when she put you down.

EVA

I did?

LOTTIE

You know you did. You were spoiled rotten.

EVA *(pleased)*

Hmmm, I don't remember that part. I just know Mama was like . . . like kinda cold. She never just reached out and hugged you. Oh, I needed that. I did. And I've never had that kind of love . . . from anybody.

LOTTIE

I know. It seemed you had to be leaving on a trip or something to get her to respond. Maybe that's why I was always leaving.

EVA

Yes, you were always away . . . like when Mama was pregnant with Ada Lou. Oh! that almost did me in. I was embarrassed to death.

LOTTIE

What on earth for?

EVA

I just was. I kinda knew where babies came from, but to think that Mama and Papa, well, you know? That she and Papa . . .

(Buries head in pillow and howls)
A-h-h-h! I don't want to think about it even now!

LOTTIE

Oh, Eva, behave!

EVA

Well, I had to live here! It was Frances Evelyn that told me about it. My goodness, I never realized. How did she know? Did Aunt Edna tell her all that? *(Exasperated)* Why, now I think of it, that was a horrible story to tell to me . . . me, just a child! You know, I think I'm going to go over there right now and give both of them a piece of my mind!

LOTTIE

You'll do nothing of the kind. You're not starting some sort of ruckus over some old hurts, so lie down.

EVA *(lays back, pouting)*

One of these days I'm gonna get even. You just wait and see.

LOTTIE *(letting out a sigh)*

There's no such thing as getting even. I wanted to get even with my mother-in-law for all the mean things she did to me, but I didn't get the chance. Now it doesn't matter.

EVA

She was a mean woman, wasn't she? When did Mrs. Kokaska die?

LOTTIE

Two years . . . two months and six days ago at 6:30 p.m. on a Thursday. And it was a hot day like this, and I hope an even hotter one in Hell when she got there!

EVA

Why, Lottie. You do go on.

LOTTIE

If it's about Mrs. Kokaska, I have no trouble doing it.

EVA

Has it made things easier between you and Karl with her gone?

LOTTIE

Somewhat, but she taught him well.

EVA

Taught him what?

LOTTIE

Things like having dinner ready the moment he sets foot in the door . . . having the kitchen floor so clean you can eat off it . . . (*Aside*) Every good Polish housewife has a spotless kitchen! And sex every night.

EVA (*stunned for a moment*)

Every night? Lottie!

LOTTIE

It would be if I couldn't find an excuse now and then, but then he's not fit to live with.

EVA (*fumbling for a cigarette*)

Oh, my God. Sex . . . every night? Why, I'm appalled. I mean, Morris and I . . . oh, Lottie, how do you let him get away with something like that? It's just not . . . not healthy!

LOTTIE

Not healthy? Oh, Eva, I like it, too!

EVA (*loud shriek*)

EEEK! I don't want to hear any more. I mean, we've never talked like this before.

LOTTIE

Then what would you say if I told you he roughs me up a bit now and then?

EVA

174

I'd say "hush your mouth!" Lottie, are you in trouble? I mean, do you need some help with this . . . this situation? We could get Earle to . . .

LOTTIE *(brushing it off)*

I was joking. It's nothing serious.

EVA

Nothing serious? How long has this been going on?

LOTTIE *(reflecting)*

Almost from the start. I think that's what attracted me to him. I always wanted someone to dominate me . . . take charge.

EVA

Really! Someone dominate you? You're too strong of a person.

LOTTIE

I really wasn't. And I was tired of pretending I was. When Karl walked into my citizenship class there at Hull House and I saw this blond, blue-eyed giant standing before me, I got all weak inside. And from that moment on, he just took over my life. And I was glad to let him do it.

EVA

How can you let him be mean to you . . . and beat up on you?

LOTTIE

Oh, Eva, I can control things. Things are fine. Karl's a good man, a good father, but he has his faults.

EVA

It sure sounds like it. But, Lottie, you're OK, aren't you? I don't like the thought of anyone laying a hand on you.

LOTTIE

Don't worry about it, Eva. I'm sorry I brought it up because he's not like that any more. But . . . he still can get a bit rough in his love making.

EVA *(mild shriek)*

Hush! I don't understand these things. I mean, if Morris . . . I mean if Morris started to knock me around, well . . . I'd . . .

LOTTIE

You'd what?

EVA

Well, you know. *(hesitates and considers)* I might at least know he's around! He's been traveling so much lately. Always finding some excuse to spend more time in New Orleans.

LOTTIE

When he's home is there a problem?

EVA *(changing the subject)*

175

I've got a headache. I'm not used to talking like this. Maybe I should get some of that nerve tonic that Doc Strawbridge whips up?

LOTTIE

Don't tell me he's still turning out that "nerve medicine."

EVA

He sure is and Lou Berta's one of his best customers, too. Oh, that's right. I'm gonna send her down there and have her get me a bottle. I would go myself, but someone might see me . . . . one of Aunt Edna's spies.

(EVA goes to the door and calls out, "Lou Berta! Yoo-hoo, Lou Berta.")

LOTTIE

Don't you need a prescription?

EVA

Shoot, no! He just dishes it out the back door for all I know.

LOTTIE

You're not really going to send Lou Berta down there, are you?

EVA

Of course! I have a headache. This has been such a bad time for me and I need to CALM my nerves! I'm not made of steel like you!

LOTTIE

I don't like this one bit!

EVA

I'm just looking after my health . . . and SANITY!

(LOU BERTA sticks her head inside the door.)

LOU BERTA

You CALLED, Miss Eva?

EVA

Yes. I need you to run a little errand for me.

LOU BERTA

Seems like that's all I been doing today . . . running up to the church, dragging those fans back. Why, I thought somebody was gonna call the law. Mrs. Gibbs came out on her porch and just glared at me like I was some thief!

EVA

Nobody thought anything of the kind. Now . . . I want you to go down to Doc Strawbridge's Drug Store and get me something.

LOU BERTA *(looks at her suspiciously)*

Get what, Miss Eva?

(EVA takes some money out of her purse and puts it in her hand.)

176

EVA

Some of his . . . tonic. It'll only take you a minute.

LOU BERTA *(in disbelief)*

Now, Miss Eva . . . what for you gonna take some of that stuff? Yo' Mama would whip you up one side of the street and down the other if she knew you even so much as thought about that tonic.

EVA

Now I don't need a lecture. Mama won't know. I just want something to settle my nerves with all that's going on around here. I feel jumpy and my head hurts.

LOTTIE

Eva . . . don't you think . . .

EVA

I NEED SOMETHING TO CALM MY NERVES! Everybody in this town takes something now and then and I don't see why I can't get just as CALM as any of them. Now, Lou Berta, will you just get it for me . . . please?

LOU BERTA *(shaking her head)*

Sho' don't like this one bit, no m'am. Once you start taking that stuff, you just can't seem to stop.

EVA

We'll see about that! I have lots of self control.

LOTTIE

Sure you do.

EVA

Now buy yourself a cone of ice cream if you want, but don't spend too much, you hear?

LOU BERTA *(exits mumbling)*

Running all over town . . . up to the church . . . down to the drug store, gotta get dinner on the table . . .

LOTTIE

You shouldn't have her running around like that.

EVA

Well, you had her toting fans from the church. This is just a little bottle of nerve tonic. I'd go myself, but it would be all over town. You know how people here talk.

LOTTIE

I have a feeling it's gonna be all over town, anyway . . . wait and see.

EVA

177

And I'm sure Aunt Edna will be the first to know!

(The door opens and ADA LOU comes in with a grave expression.)

ADA LOU

I think you'd better come in. I don't know what to do. Mama can't seem to get her breath.

(LOTTIE heads out the door immediately. EVA hangs back and fumbles for another cigarette as she starts to cry.)

ACT ONE

SCENE THREE

(Later in the afternoon. The sleeping porch is empty as the lights come up. Enter ADA LOU and EVA, exhausted. EVA collapses on the bed, ADA LOU stands looking through the blinds.)

ADA LOU

I still think we should've taken Mama to the hospital in Birmingham. I don't care what Dr. Sizemore said. They'd be able to do more for her than we can. I mean, I don't know what to do when she gets those spells where she can't breathe? I don't have any nurse's training! And . . . it scares me to death!

EVA *(still battling the heat)*

Ada Lou, Dr. Sizemore's right. It wouldn't help at all at this point. They can't do any more in Birmingham than we can do right here . . . and you know how Mama hates a hospital. Only thing we can do is to make sure she's comfortable and not in any pain. Oh . . . pain! I don't want no pain . . . can't take it . . . Ada Lou . . .

(Sits on bed and pats the side, indicating for ADA LOU to sit.)

This breast cancer thing of Mama's. Do you think it's inherited? I mean, will any of us be going through this? I tried talking to my doctor in Mobile, but he didn't know much of anything at all about breast cancer. Nobody seems to.

ADA LOU

I haven't really been concerned about it . . . until now. When Mama had both breasts removed ten years ago, I thought that was the end of it. But apparently something can flare up on down the line. But none of Mama's sisters have had it. Aunt Edna doesn't, for all I know.

EVA *(in spiteful manner)*

Well, I'm sure we all would know if Aunt Edna had it. That would be the case of the century! Oh . . . I remember when Mama had her breasts removed. I didn't understand it! I was just devastated when I found out and couldn't be there with her. *(Pensively)* We'd just lost Alice. I couldn't think

178

. . . couldn't go anywhere or see anybody. I just stayed home with the curtains drawn. Morris got real worried at that time. He wanted us to drive up the Grove Park Hotel in Asheville and spend some time in the mountains . . . away from the seashore, but I just couldn't get out of my room. And when the news came about Mama, well, I thought, literally, I was just gonna die right there. Oh, Ada Lou, honey . . . I don't know what we would have done if you hadn't taken charge . . . seems like you're always doing that, doesn't it? You're an angel, darling. A real angel. I just sat in the room, crying my eyes out over Alice . . . and Mama. I thought my life was over, too.

(She goes over and puts an arm around ADA LOU.)

Ada Lou, you take more after Mama than me or Lottie put together. I mean about being able to handle pain and all sorts of trials. I'm just not that strong. I just can't handle pain . . . and disappointments.

(ADA LOU is a bit flustered at the sentiment being expressed. She quickly changes the subject.)

ADA LOU

Oh, I wish Earle were here. I'm getting so concerned about not hearing from him. He should be here right now! I told Mr. Wheeler down at the draft board to find out who his commanding officer over at Fort Gordon is 'cause I'm gonna call him myself and find out what's going on. Heavens! I've known soldiers who've gotten passes to come home if their Mama's had a bad cold! And here . . .

EVA *(softly)*

Hush, now. Don't get yourself in a snit. I'm sure they're doing the best they can to get Earle here.

ADA LOU *(gets up and paces nervously)*

Mr. Wheeler said there was some sort of delay in letting him go. I don't know what that's all about. Somehow I feel uneasy about the whole thing . . . like something is going on. I don't know what, but I seem to know when something is going wrong with Earle.

EVA

Oh, I'm sure he's all right . . .

ADA LOU

No . . . I feel something is going on. He's just kinda stopped writing to me . . . and to Mama. I found a letter on Mama's bureau and it seems to be the last one she's had. It was written almost three weeks ago! Earle doesn't do that kind of thing. He's either in touch with Mama or me . . .

EVA *(trying to calm her)*

Maybe they're on . . . what'cha call it . . . maneuvering? Something like that . . . out there shooting at one another.

ADA LOU

No . . . he's finished with that. In fact, in his last letter he said that he might be stationed right there at Fort Gordon for a while . . . and not have to go overseas. Oh, I'd be happy to hear that. He mentioned something about how his new sergeant has gotten him a spot that would start right after his basic training. (*ADA LOU keeps pacing, then stops.*) I do hope so . . . I'd just die if something happened to Earle . . . or to Hershal . . . but I feel so protective towards Earle . . . always have, you know that. And thank goodness I have a husband who understand that. I don't quite understand it myself.

EVA

Honey, blood relationships are much stronger and lasting than any married relationship. I know that for a fact! You and Earle have always been close and it will always be that way. Mark my words.

ADA LOU

Yes . . . we have been close. I feel like I practically raised him from a baby, but oh, it wasn't that way at first. I was so jealous! I was so used to having Mama all to myself I was infuriated when he was born. (*Laughs to herself*) I hate to admit it, but I looked upon you and Lottie as my aunts, not sisters . . . because of the age differences, you know. And, too, both of you were always gone, which let me have Mama all to myself. Then Earle came along and that changed everything. You know, I was only eleven years old, but I had an idea where babies came from and I was mortified to think that . . . well, Mama and Papa . . .

EVA (excited)

You were! Why, Ada Lou! It was the same with me when you were born! Lord, I was so embarrassed to think that Mama and Papa were . . . well, you know . . . carrying on . . . Whooee! Well . . . well . . . I don't feel so bad now. Come here, sister dear, and give me a big hug! (*They embrace.*) Oh, this family has so many levels . . . doesn't it? Me and Lottie . . . then you came. You . . . then Earle. We're really two different families, aren't we? Mama sure had a sense of timing, didn't she?

(*Enter LOTTIE.*)

LOTTIE

Lou Berta's back from town . . . she brought this to you, Eva . . . and some change. She's very upset, you know, about you making her do this.

(*EVA grabs the bottle.*)

EVA

Oh . . . well . . .

ADA LOU

What is it?

EVA

Oh . . . nothing. Just a little tonic . . . .

ADA LOU

Eva . . . you didn't?

EVA

It's nothing . . . nothing . . . nothing! I just feel like I needed a little pick-me-up.

(ADA LOU takes bottle and examines it closely.)

ADA LOU

So this is the infamous Doc Strawbridge's Nerve Tonic. I didn't believe you would do it.

EVA

I don't need a lecture from anyone. *(She takes the bottle.)* I just felt like with so much going on I needed something to calm me down . . . why, everybody takes this stuff . . . Lord knows what's in it . . . but I don't see where I am any different from anyone else, especially in view of the circumstances. I could have called that old bootlegger over at the state line, but I haven't had a drink of liquor since I left the University of Alabama in 1922 . . . and you can thank Papa for that. Oh, don't think there haven't been times when I needed a drink, what with Alice and all that . . . but I didn't violate my oath . . . and I'm not breaking it now. BUT I NEED TO GET CALM!

LOTTIE

Nobody's faulting you . . . it's OK . . . just relax . . .

(Eva clasps the bottle to her breast.)

EVA

I just want to try it. That's all . . . it's probably vile!

ADA LOU

How do you take the stuff? Do you just swig it right from the bottle?

EVA *(squints at the label)*

No . . . it says four tablespoons with water.

LOTTIE

Four tablespoons! My god, that might knock you out for a week.

EVA

Ada Lou, hon . . . why don't you get me a spoon and some glasses from the kitchen? Let's all try it.

ADA LOU

Oh, no . . . Not me. But I'll get you a glass and a spoon . . . *(Exits)*

LOTTIE

Eva . . . be careful. You don't know what's in that . . . that potion. I mean,

181

everyone knows Doc Strawbridge is not even a licensed pharmacist . . . he just runs the drug store. I suppose he can order anything he wants, but there's no telling what's in that so-called "nerve medicine!"

EVA

Oh, it's nothing . . . nothing at all. Lou Berta told me once it was the best there was for rheumatism . . . she says old Miz Pointer up there on the hill swears by it. And if Miz Pointer puts her seal of approval on something, then it's OK . . .

(ADA LOU enters with tray.)

ADA LOU

I want to see this . . . the very idea!

EVA

Well, I declare . . . everybody's making such a fuss over nothing at all. Here, give that to me . . .

(She takes the tray and puts it on the table between the beds. She measures the four generous tablespoons, glancing from time to time at the two ladies, and then pours in some water. She swirls it around, smells it and holds it up to the light.)

It's nothing special . . . really. Here goes!

(As EVA downs the mixture, ADA LOU and LOTTIE are spellbound. EVA grimaces, but then smacks her lips appreciatively.)

It tastes like some kinda cough syrup . . . what is it?

(EVA smacks her lips, takes another sip.)

No, it tastes like . . . something like Fletcher's Castoria!

(She continues to smack her lips.)

But not quite . . . here, Lottie, you taste.

LOTTIE

I don't think so . . .

EVA

Oh, come on . . . just a sip . . . it's not bad.

(LOTTIE reluctantly takes the glass and smells the contents.)

LOTTIE

Does it need more water?

EVA

No . . . you don't need any water . . . just take a sip. Here . . . let's pour in some more.

(As EVA pours a generous amount, LOTTIE exchanges looks with ADA LOU, then shrugs and takes a sip. Nothing registers at first, then she sinks down on the bed, handing the glass to EVA.)

LOTTIE
Wow! That packs a kick . . . o-o-o-o!

ADA LOU
I don't believe this . . . you both are acting crazy! What is in that stuff?

EVA
Oh . . . it doesn't matter. Here . . . try it. It's good.

> *(EVA hands the glass to ADA LOU and then twirls around, arms spread out.)*

In fact . . . it's divine!!

ACT ONE

SCENE FOUR

> *(Twilight on the sleeping porch. The floor lamp is on. ADA LOU is propped up in bed at stage left. LOTTIE appears to have passed out in the chair. EVA is waltzing around the room making huge circles in the air with the cord from her kimono. She is obviously tipsy and shrieks as the lights go up.)*

EVA *(almost stumbling)*
Remember how Ginger Rogers in that movie . . . what was it . . . "Flying Down to Rio" . . . how she had this white boa that just seemed to hang in the air every time she turned . . .

> *(She twirls around in a dance.)*

but those damn . . . oops! 'scuse me . . . darn feathers were floating all over the place like a . . . like a plucked chicken . . .

> *(She clucks like a chicken and flaps her arms in drunken silliness. LOTTIE shields her ears and massages her temples, indicating a terrible headache. DIEDRE's voice is heard at the door.)*

DIEDRE
Mama . . . can I come in?

> *(ADA LOU raises up from her bed, then sinks back down, cradling her head in her arms. Only EVA seems to be off in another world enjoying herself.)*

ADA LOU *(speaks to the door)*
Oh, Dee . . . I thought you were over at Jimmie Ann's house. No . . . don't come in . . . you go on back over there. *(To the room in general)* Oh, my head . . . I think it's about to come off! What is in that tonic?? OH!

> *(She sinks back in bed, pulling a pillow over her face.)*

DIEDRE

Mama . . . I'm afraid to walk back over there in the dark. I'm afraid of snakes . . . and Jimmie Ann says they're lots of them out there in the bushes.

ADA LOU

Dee . . . I can't help you now . . . but there aren't any snakes out there. Just stay on the walk. Now go on back to Frances Evelyn's and I'll be over to say good night . . . later, oh, my!

DIEDRE

But, Mama . . . I want to come in . . .

ADA LOU *(harshly)*

DIEDRE! Please . . . please hold down the noise! I've told you that your Mam-Ma is not well and I have a sick headache. *(to herself)* Oh, do I have a headache!

> *(EVA lets out more chicken sounds and picks up the tonic bottle and takes another swig. DIEDRE sticks her head in the door to see what's going on.)*

DIEDRE

But yawl are making more noise than me!

ADA LOU

DIEDRE! I don't want to have to tell you again! Now just go on back . . . this room is for grown ladies only. You know that. No children allowed!

DIEDRE

Yes, M'am.

> *(Takes a last look around, then slowly closes the door.)*

ADA LOU

Oh . . . my head is about to split open . . . why did I ever let you talk me into having some of that . . . that tonic!

> *(Livelier than ever, EVA picks up the bottle and turns it upside down. At this point, she might go through all sorts of motions, like sucking on the bottle to get the last drop . . . or pouring more water into the bottle and swishing it around to get one more jolt.)*

EVA

I kinda l-i-k-e this stuff! I wonder if we can get some more! You think the store is still open?

> *(LOTTIE stirs in her chair and gets a bit sober.)*

LOTTIE

Eva . . . you've had enough . . . we all have. I don't know what's in it, but it's about to make me crawl in bed and stay for a solid month! Oh, my head!

EVA

Oh, don't be such sticks in the mud.

(She stops short and her eyes grow wide. She starts sticking out her chest and examining it with her hands.)

Oh! I think it's making my boobies bigger!

(She starts strutting around with a mimicking walk.)

I feel like I'm Mae West! Watch this. "If you've got five dollars, come up and see me some time . . . big boy!" Who-o-o!

(Suddenly, ADA LOU and LOTTIE see the hilarity in the situation and they break out in peals of laughter, falling out of bed, etc. Enter AUNT EDNA, who stands there like a prison guard surveying the scene. Dressed in a simple house dress, but wearing a hat and white gloves, she carries along with her purse, a cardboard sign in child's handwriting that reads: "Quiet Three Ladies Laughing." Seeing AUNT EDNA, the ladies sober up immediately as the room becomes absolutely still.)

AUNT EDNA

What is going on here . . . pray tell? *(No reply)* My sister is lying in there across the hall on her deathbed and you're all in here just having a party! Having a good time! Why, I could hear you all the way up to the church! The very idea! What will people say! Laughing . . . while your mother is dying!

(No one dares speak.)

What on earth could be funny?!

(She turns over the sign and reads it aloud.)

"Quiet . . . three ladies laughing." And . . . who did this? Who hung this on the door? What kind of game is this?

(Almost falling over, EVA wobbles over and takes the sign from AUNT EDNA and looks it over.)

EVA

Lor-r-d . . . that Diedre did this. I swanee! That chi-ld . . . *(drunken giggle)* Wh-y-y she's as smart as a whip-p-p!

(AUNT EDNA sniffs the air with suspicion.)

AUNT EDNA

I don't find anything funny about this at all! I don't know what's going on here, but I want you to know one thing. I have just come from choir practice . . . which, by the way . . . we had to cancel . . . because SOMEBODY stole the choir fans!

(EVA and ADA LOU look to LOTTIE.)

I have it on good authority . . . from Mrs. Gibbs, no less . . . that it was Lou

185

Berta! She saw her coming out of the church this very afternoon dragging two fans up the street! Why, I was embarrassed to death . . . for the family's sake, of course. Is that true? Did Lou Berta take our choir fans? I'm sure one of you (*staring at EVA*) put her up to it! Now where are they?

LOTTIE

Yes . . . the fans are here . . . in Mama's room. I sent Lou Berta up there to get them because I didn't think they would be used until Sunday . . . and it was like an oven in Mama's room.

AUNT EDNA (*very smug and self-righteous*)

That's not like you, Lottie, but then I guess you Catholics up there in Chicago can just walk into your synagogue and take whatever you want whenever you want it. We don't do things like that down here . . . if you remember your training at all. Now, I think you owe the whole choir an apology for disrupting our practice . . .

LOTTIE

I think not . . . and besides, we don't call our churches synagogues. I was just looking out for Mama and her needs and I thought about those fans not being used until at least Sunday. You have fans galore and I haven't seen you offering any for Mama's use during this heat wave. No . . . I don't feel any need to apologize to any of those ole crows in choir!

EVA (*a whoop of laughter*)

That's right! There's no need to apologize to a bunch of old crows! We were thinking of Mama!

(*EVA definitely staggers a bit, and it does not go unnoticed by AUNT EDNA, who starts circling her and studying her with care. Then she stiffens.*)

AUNT EDNA

Just as I thought . . . YOU'RE DRUNK! All of you!

(*The three ladies jump as though shot.*)

EVA

Drunk! . . . (*EVA moves unsteadily towards AUNT EDNA, menacingly.*) I've never been DRUNK in my whole life . . . and I'm not drunk now . . . you ole biddie!

ADA LOU (*moves to restrain EVA*)

Eva . . . don't make a scene . . .

LOTTIE

Aunt Edna . . . that's unfair. We have not been drinking. We've been under a strain . . .

AUNT EDNA (*adamant*)

You're drunk . . . all of you! And I know it! I can't believe it! Lula's dying

186

in there and you three girls are cavorting around in here like it was a circus or something.

LOTTIE
Aunt Edna . . . please. We have not been drinking . . . now stop that.

AUNT EDNA
Oh . . . don't tell me! You've been drinking . . . oh—

(Singling out EVA and shaking a finger at her)
Oh, you don't fool me one bit, young lady. Why, you've been tippling ever since you were over at the university!

(EVA explodes in a rage! Screeching like a banshee and holding one of her slippers aloft, she lunges across the room at AUNT EDNA.)

EVA
E-e-e-e! You . . . you ole BITCH!

(Pandemonium ensues! LOTTIE grabs EVA as ADA LOU races to shield AUNT EDNA from the attack. AUNT EDNA is already traumatized by the outburst.)

AUNT EDNA
Oh! . . . Heavens! Let me out of here!

(LOTTIE continues to restrain EVA, who is fighting mad.)

LOTTIE
Eva . . . for God's sake . . . Stop it!

(EVA and AUNT EDNA are kept apart. Things calm down.)

EVA *(in a frenzy)*
You've always accused me of some sort of vile thing . . . you . . . mean ole . . . BAT!

AUNT EDNA
Oh . . . let me out of here . . . I'm going to faint!

(AUNT EDNA collapses against ADA LOU, who steers her towards one of the beds to lie down. AUNT EDNA mumbles incoherently.)
Water . . . I need a glass of water . . .

(EVA pauses in her attack, looking vindicated and still full of mischief. LOU BERTA sticks her head inside the door to see what is going on and is spotted by LOTTIE.)

LOTTIE
Quick! . . . Lou Berta! . . . bring a glass of water.

(LOU BERTA shrugs and exits. EVA defiantly whips out a cigarette and lights it with a flourish. She then starts sashaying up and down in front of AUNT EDNA like a hussy or streetwalker.)

ADA LOU

Eva! Please . . . you've started enough already!

EVA *(unconcerned)*

Oh, real-ly? I'm not doing anything that's not normal . . . FOR ME! EVERYONE knows I'm an old SOT! . . . and that I smoke like a Chinaman!

(AUNT EDNA raises herself up in bed, but when she sees EVA smoking, she lets out an audible moan and sinks back down.)

AUNT EDNA

What is my crime? I just don't understand it . . . All my life I've tried to keep our family's reputation above questioning . . . and what happens? *(Pointing an accusing finger at EVA.)* I am turned upon and physically assaulted by my own niece! And then PERSONALLY insulted with such vile names that only . . . only COMMON people would use. Oh, I'm so glad Lula didn't witness this spectacle. She's tried so hard with you, young lady . . .

EVA

I'm sure your precious Frances Evelyn would never have acted like this . . . is that what you're saying?

(AUNT EDNA becomes defiant. She sits up in bed, then stands up slowly, eying EVA the whole time.)

AUNT EDNA

Of course she wouldn't! She's a true MOLLOY . . . AND . . . a GALLOWAY.

(She stands there, shoulders thrown back, looking down her nose at EVA.)

You're pure NOLAN, young lady. There's not a drop of MOLLOY blood in you, from all appearances!

(EVA storms over and gets right in AUNT EDNA's face, very menacingly.)

EVA

What-in-the-HELL is that supposed to mean? Mama was never stuck up about being a MOLLOY! What is so great about that?

AUNT EDNA

Don't you curse me, young lady! I've had more than I can take for one evening. I'm not going to stand for any more sass or backtalk from you. I've had enough, and I'm beginning not to know you at all!

(She looks around for her belongings and appears in a hurry to get out of the room.)

Where's my purse? Where's my hat?

EVA *(steps in to block her way)*

Pure Nolan, huh? You never liked Papa, did you? You always thought Mama

188

married beneath herself, didn't you! DIDN'T YOU?

(She doesn't wait for an answer. She's off and running.)

Well, I don't really care whether you thought Papa measured up to your standards, but I can tell you one thing . . . he was head and shoulders above that lying, cheating shyster lawyer you married!

(AUNT EDNA is almost too stunned for words. She turns to walk off in a huff, but then turns and faces EVA head on.)

AUNT EDNA

No . . . I never did like your father. I won't give you such an opinion on Sam Nolan as you gave me about my dear husband. I love my sister dearly, but I'll never know what Lula saw in him. But, I know one thing . . . you are a mirror image of him, young lady!

EVA

I knew it! *(To LOTTIE and ADA LOU)* See there! Didn't I tell you she's always had it in for me when I have done nothing . . . not one thing evil to her. Oh, doesn't that just take the cake?

AUNT EDNA

This is not the time . . . nor the place . . . to discuss this any further. I'm not used to being involved in SCENES. But one day, young lady, I'll tell you a thing or two about Sam Nolan, and I guarantee you won't be up there on such a high horse any more. Now, excuse me. I'm going in to be with my sister. *(She starts for the door.)*

ADA LOU *(letting out a scream)*

Earle!

(Standing in the doorway in a disheveled, ill-fitted suit with his nose all bloodied is a startled young man. Everyone in the room is dumbstruck and perplexed. ADA LOU composes herself and then runs to embrace him. No one else makes a move.)

Earle! Why . . . what's the matter? Have you been in an accident?

(EARLE doesn't answer. He looks from face to face and appears stunned. LOU BERTA enters, wiping her eyes with the corner of her apron.)

LOU BERTA

Y'awl just hush all this here fussing and fighting. Lawd help us! While y'awl were screaming and hollering in here, Miss Lula . . . well . . . she's gone.

AUNT EDNA

Oh, no . . . Lula!

EVA

Mama?

(EVA heads for the door, distraught. AUNT EDNA starts for the door,

189

too, but EVA pushes her out of the way.)

Mama! *(louder)* MAMA! *(EVA exits.)*

(Other family members assume various poses of grief. EARLE walks to center stage and stares out into the audience, then breaks into tears. ADA LOU comes up from behind and buries her head on his shoulder.)

ACT TWO

SCENE ONE

(Late evening. EARLE NOLAN sits on the front steps, nursing a glass of iced tea while fiddling with a small "Man in Service" flag that used to hang in the front window. He's changed into looser, better fitting clothes. From time to time he dabs at his nose with a handkerchief. EARLE is troubled. A dog barks in the distance and a train whistle can be heard. LOU BERTA appears at the screen door, then pushes it open.)

LOU BERTA

Mr. Earle . . . I'm getting ready to leave. You want something 'fore I go? Gonna be lots of folks here tomorrow . . . lots going on and I've been running all day. Needs to get my rest.

EARLE

No, no . . . I'm fine. Run on home.

LOU BERTA *(hesitant)*

Mr. Earle . . . some'm ain't right, is it? How come you got yo nose all messed up . . . and where'd you get them clothes you got off the train in? They ain't Army clothes. I know that. I don't like none of this. No-o-o sir-ree . . .

EARLE

Not now, Lou Berta. Let's not talk about it now.

LOU BERTA

I sho' don't like seeing you this way. It ain't like you.

(EARLE gets up off the steps and goes over and holds LOU BERTA by both arms.)

EARLE

Tomorrow. Let's talk tomorrow. I don't feel like talking just now. I was sitting thinking about all the times we spent on this front porch. Mama . . . I barely remember Papa . . .

(EARLE buries his head in her bosom and LOU BERTA's arms envelop him.)

190

LOU BERTA

Those were good times . . . but they weren't without trouble. No such thing being no trouble around . . . it's just there . . . with the good times . . .

(EARLE holds back his tears and then straightens up. LOU BERTA pats his back concerned and then EARLE breaks away.)

EARLE

It's going to be hard, isn't it . . . I don't like thinking about what's ahead.

LOU BERTA

Plenty of time to think about what's ahead. Why don't you go up to your room and go to bed . . . I done fluffed up that feather bed for you since I know you been sleeping on those hard old Army beds. Do you good to get back in yo' own bed . . .

EARLE

I suppose it will. Now . . . YOU run along and get in YOUR bed. You're no spring chicken any more . . .

LOU BERTA

That sho' is the truth . . . it sho' is . . . I'll be in early and have yo' favorite pancakes fixed for breakfast. I got the biscuits soaking in buttermilk right now. Now you go on up, you hear?

(LOU BERTA goes back inside and EARLE sits back down on the steps. ADA LOU slowly comes out on the porch, then walks over and sits beside him.)

ADA LOU

It's still hot, isn't it? Wish we had just a shower to cool things off before tomorrow.

(ADA LOU wraps one arm around him.)

ADA LOU

Diedre was thrilled to see you. I don't think she quite understands that her Mam-Ma is gone. Oh, if something happens to Hershal I don't know if I could tell her. Or, for that matter, if something happened to you.

(ADA LOU hugs him and kisses him on the ear.)
I'm so glad you're finally here . . .

(EARLE somewhat pulls away from her grasp, leaving ADA LOU a bit perplexed.)

ADA LOU *(quietly)*

I was really getting worried about you.We've had no word from you for weeks . . . *(EARLE doesn't answer.)* We sent a wire to your commanding officer . . . or rather Mr. Wheeler down at the draft board did. He even called him direct when we still heard nothing from you.

EARLE

Oh . . . so that's why he was down at the train.

ADA LOU

Mr. Wheeler? Was he down at the train?

EARLE

Oh, yeah, he was there all right. Yeah! That makes everything perfectly clear now. (*EARLE dabs at his nose.*)

ADA LOU

Makes what clear?

EARLE

Why he punched me in the nose . . .

ADA LOU

Mr. Wheeler hit you? What on earth . . .

EARLE

He said that's what Papa would have done . . . or even worse.

ADA LOU

You're not making sense, Earle.

EARLE

He hit me because he knew . . . he knew about me . . . about my being in the stockade!

ADA LOU

In a stockade? Earle . . . What are you talking about?

EARLE

I was in the stockade. The Fort Gordon stockade.

ADA LOU *(perplexed)*

The what?

EARLE

The stockade . . . the jail . . . the place where they put military criminals . . . and unsavory persons.

ADA LOU *(in great anguish)*

Oh . . . Earle . . . You're not in some kind of trouble . . . are you?

EARLE *(quietly)*

I was for a while there . . . I'm not at this moment. But, who knows. I've got a feeling that the real trouble is just beginning. Oh, Ada Lou, don't push me too far right now. I can't sort it all out at this point.

ADA LOU

You're not making any sense. Here . . . *(She pats a space next to her on the steps.)* Come . . . sit down . . . tell me what's going on, but don't wake Eva or Lottie. They've both had a hard time sleeping since they've been here and are just exhausted. Come here . . . sit down. You're talking gibberish. I want to understand what's happening.

(EARLE sits next to her, still twirling the flag. He looks at it closely.)

EARLE

Mama's gonna have to get . . . aw shoot! I've got to stop referringto Mama to fix things. I was gonna say Mama oughta get a new flag with a gold star on it to indicate her son is dead! Missing in action! Ca-poo-toe, as my sergeant used to say . . . *(softly)* used to say.

ADA LOU *(quietly)*

Dead? Earle . . . look at me. What is going on? I don't like the way you're talking.

EARLE *(matter-of-fact)*

Ada Lou, I have gone over this thing in my mind for days . . . thinking I could at least explain it to you, but now that I'm home . . . I . . . I just don't know how to tell you . . . or anyone for that matter. There's just no way to explain it all! It just happened. *(EARLE jumps up.)* Jesus! I can't make it sound right . . . any way I try. Oh, Lordy, Lordy, Lordy . . .

(He sits down again on the steps, bending his head to his knees in anguish.)

Oh, Ada Lou . . . it's serious . . . more serious than I thought. And now being here . . . at Mama's it takes on a different meaning.

ADA LOU *(greatly concerned)*

It's all right . . . all right . . . Tell me. I've learned that I can accept almost anything . . . except lying and murder. It can't be worse than that . . . can it?

EARLE *(quietly)*

Lots worse, Ada Lou. I'm not in the Army any more. I've been discharged . . . let go!

(ADA LOU is shocked and starts to say something.)

No . . . don't say anything just now . . . just let me talk it out. This isn't easy for me to do. *(Hesitates, then plunges in.)* I've been court-martialed . . . kicked out the Army.

(ADA LOU struggles to say something, but Earle still hushes her.)

Shhhh . . . Please . . . Let me finish it . . . *(Composes himself)* I have been discharged in a less than honorable manner . . . LESS THAN HONORABLE . . . which means they've put a label on me for life that I'll never be able to lose. And that's it in a nutshell. *(He gets up from the steps.)* I don't know where I stand right now on anything . . . Ha! I don't even think I can vote! But I won't have to worry about that . . . not for another couple of years. Oh, there's so much going on with this thing . . . so much I don't know about. Of course the draft board was notified right away and that's

193

why old man Wheeler was down there at the train since he was Papa's best friend. I guess he thought it was his manly duty to whip my ass! Boy! He was out to get me, all right. He kept shouting how Papa would be disgraced if he were alive. I'm sure everyone in town either saw it, or has heard about it by now. *(Turns pleading to ADA LOU)* BUT PAPA'S DEAD AND I'M THE ONE WHO HAS TO LIVE WITH THIS!

(He wads up the flag and tosses it into the bushes.)

ADA LOU

Earle, please . . . what have you done?

EARLE *(sits down in great anguish)*

Oh, God!

(Big sobs. ADA LOU puts her arms around him and rocks him gently.)

I was in the brig when I got word about Mama not being able to last much longer. That's why they hurried up the court martial. I was so upset, because I didn't realize how bad she was. And then it dawned on me, if she died before I got out of the stockade, she would never know anything about this! Nothing at all! For a moment there I was happy! Yes, happy . . . in spite of all I had been through. My tears just burst out like a dam breaking and all those guys in the cells around me started hooting . . . and hollering and jeering me. They thought I was crying over what I had done, but that wasn't it. I was praying as hard as I could that Mama wouldn't never hear a word of this.

(He cries a little, softly, as ADA LOU rocks him. She waits for him to gain composure.)

ADA LOU

Earle, whatever you've done can't be as bad as wishing Mama dead! You haven't murdered anyone, have you? Listen to me . . . whatever you have done, I won't blame you. You're still my baby brother.

EARLE

I won't go into details . . . I couldn't do it if I wanted to . . . because . . . because any way I try to explain it . . . it just doesn't sound right. And you're the only one I wanted to tell. I couldn't explain it to Eva or Lottie . . . I just couldn't. You'll have to explain it to Lottie and Eva . . . I couldn't do that. *(He clears his throat again, and begins rather matter-of-fact.)* No, I didn't murder anyone . . . I did something much worse. I fell in love . . . fell in love with someone in my outfit. We were caught in a compromising situation . . . on leave . . . by the M.P.'s. We were thrown in the stockade and then court-martialed. That's it pure and simple and that's about as much as I would like to say about it at this point, except to say I was stripped of my uniform . . . my dignity . . . and given that rotten suit of clothes I wore in here this afternoon. I felt like a criminal getting out of prison. Jesus! I felt so . . . so degraded!

(A dead silence)

ADA LOU *(trying to comprehend)*

Oh, Earle . . . Earle . . .

EARLE

I almost didn't come at all, because I didn't want to cause anyone any embarrassment. I at least got to tell you first hand before the story got around. So, I've decided it would be too hard on everyone, even for me, to attend the funeral. That's why I'm taking that early train to Birmingham this morning. I'm not staying for the funeral. I've said my goodbyes to Mama already. It's best I just leave.

(He walks up on the porch and looks into the house. ADA LOU is stunned.)

I wanted to see this old place one more time . . . cause I know I'm not going to be coming back for a l-o-n-g time, if at all. I know that now. You know how people are. They'll talk about this forever.

ADA LOU *(hesitantly)*

Oh, Earle . . . I don't know what to say. I don't understand this . . . LOVE? You fell in love . . . with another soldier?

EARLE *(a bit upset with her)*

Ada Lou, I can't to go into it any more than what I just told you.Don't you see . . . I really don't understand it myself. Nothing like this ever happened to me before! It all came about so fast I haven't really sorted it all out . . . But, you know what . . . it seemed natural at the time. Like it was supposed to happen . . . don't ask me why. Please. *(Almost to himself)* WHY . . . WHY . . . WHY! I've never felt that way about anyone before . . . but I felt love for—

(Almost says the name, but catches himself)

—for him . . . not in the same way I feel about you . . . or Mama . . . or Papa, or for that matter, Eva and Lottie. This is something separate . . . it's something about caring for someone . . . completely. It's the exact opposite of everything I was brought up to believe about caring for someone! And it doesn't seem wrong or even dirty as some people seem to think! *(He paces.)* But, I tell'ya . . . I'm gonna find out what it's all about . . . I'm gonna have to, because there's no going back for me now. It's like I'm starting out all over again learning things about life. And now with no Mama . . . no Papa . . . I need you . . . I need some anchor . . . someone I care about from this life . . . and someone who cares about me because, Ada Lou, I'm not sure I can handle all this.

ADA LOU

Oh, Earle . . . who else was involved in this?

EARLE

I told you . . . I've said all I am going to say for the time being . . . I will sometime, but not now . . . not now.

195

ADA LOU *(gets up and paces)*

I can't take this all in . . . it's just too much . . . too much to think about. And now I feel like I've just lost you . . . and I don't want to do that.

(EARLE comes behind her and puts his arms around her.)

EARLE

You haven't lost me, Ada Lou . . . but there's nothing for you to do right now and when you get right down to it, it has nothing to do with you . . .

ADA LOU *(breaking away)*

It has everything to do with me! With all of us! Oh, Earle . . . what is family for, but to help? . . . to do something!

EARLE *(a bit disgusted)*

Do something? There's nothing for you to do . . . it's been done . . . it's over! I just don't want you of all people to turn your back on me. Ada Lou, this is something I've got to figure out by myself. I've got to understand what I am going to do from right now . . . this moment . . . and what I am going to do for the rest of my life. I can't do it from here. Couldn't put up with all the talk behind my back. All those jokes, the snickering. That's no way to live. We don't have Papa's store any more, so there's nothing here for me . . . especially with Mama gone. *(Pauses to take stock)* I suppose Mama left the house to all of us . . . I certainly don't want it keep it. I won't be coming back. Just sell it . . . and give me my share and you won't have to deal with me any more on that.

ADA LOU

That's just it . . . I don't want EVERYTHING to be over . . . Mama . . . now you. I can't live with that! I can't live with you not being a part of my life any more.

EARLE

I will still be a part of your life, but it won't be here . . . in this place. It'll be from someplace else.

ADA LOU *(slowly paces the porch)*

Where y'gonna be . . . where can I get in touch with you?

EARLE

Right now . . . I suppose New York City.

ADA LOU

Will you be with . . . that person? That person from the army?

EARLE *(hesitant)*

Yes . . . for the time being.

ADA LOU

You don't sound certain about it . . .

EARLE *(quietly)*

I'm not certain about a lot of things right now. I have no idea where all this will lead . . . I don't know what I'm going to be doing . . . with the war on I don't know how a person in my status can even get a job. I can't plan my life right now . . . it's too new! I need time to work it out . . .

ADA LOU

Oh, I don't know if I can handle you going away like this. Now with Mama gone . . . it's all too big of a change . . . too sudden . . . oh, Earle, promise me that you will write me as soon as you get settled. I don't think I can bear it if I don't know where you are . . . and how you are doing. Promise me . . . please?

EARLE *(wrapping his arms around her)*

Shhh . . . I will. Don't worry. I didn't know for sure after I told you that you would want me to be in touch.

ADA LOU

Don't ever say that . . . I mean it . . . I still have to look out for you . . .

(They stand there rocking to and fro. EARLE looks at his watch and pulls away.)

EARLE

I've gotta be going now. I've already packed some things I want you to send to me later on. Not now. Not until I'm settled.

(ADA LOU starts to say something.)

Now . . . hush a minute . . . I can't stay. I told you that. I'm gonna be on that train to Birmingham . . . *(He hesitates.)* You can tell Eva and Lottie whatever you want . . . I'll tell them when I am more sure about myself. I know this is a sneaky way out, but I don't see any point in trying to set things right just now. Besides, I don't feel as close to them as I do to you. I've counted on you to understand. I think you do, but I'm not sure they would. And, at this point, I don't want to start a commotion. Anyway, the best place for me to be right now is away from here . . . far away.

(He kisses ADA LOU on the forehead.)

Take care . . . wish me luck . . .

(EARLE grabs a small bag from the porch and dashes off. ADA LOU sinks down into a porch chair, crying softly.)

ACT TWO

SCENE TWO

(Stage light comes on, showing dawn breaking. ADA LOU is asleep in the chair or lounge. EVA appears at the screen door in a housecoat, hair in scarf and holding a cup of coffee. She loosens her robe because of the

197

early heat and then walks over to sit on the front step. Spotting ADA LOU asleep she is startled.)

EVA *(surprised)*

Oh . . . My God, Ada Lou! You almost scared me to death!

(ADA LOU stirs awake. She stretches and then sinks back into the chair, only to jump up, startled.)

ADA LOU

Oh . . . what time is it?

EVA

Must be almost 5:30 . . . I couldn't sleep a wink. I had bad dreams . . . bad . . . heard all sorts of mumbling in the night. I looked into Earle's room and it doesn't look like his bed's been slept in.

ADA LOU *(sits up and stretches)*

It wasn't. He's gone.

EVA

Gone? Earle? Well, what about the funeral today? He didn't have to get back to camp this soon, did he? *(Eva starts to go in the house.)*

ADA LOU

Well . . . he's gone now. He couldn't stay.

EVA *(with disbelief)*

I don't believe this! Not being here for the funeral!

ADA LOU

He couldn't stay . . . he had to go.

EVA

Couldn't stay? I know there's a war on, but they could do without Earle for one more day. Why didn't you wake me? Did he say goodbye to Lottie?

ADA LOU

No . . . he really didn't want to see anyone. Oh, Eva, I'm tired. I fell asleep here in this chair and I'm stiff as a board. I'd better check on Dee . . .

EVA

Now wait a minute. I don't understand one word of this. Earle must be coming back later? Right?

ADA LOU *(resigned)*

No . . . he won't be coming back today . . . or tomorrow. He's in a bit of trouble.

EVA

Trouble? What kind of trouble?

(ADA LOU takes her time. Taking the cup from EVA, she takes a sip.)

ADA LOU

He's been let go from the Army. Discharged.

EVA

Discharged? Why . . . is there something wrong with him? Was he injured?

ADA LOU *(hedging)*

No . . . but he's gotten into some sort of trouble and they've let him go.

EVA *(very concerned)*

Let him go? The Army just doesn't let people g-o-o-o. What on earth did he do?

ADA LOU

I'm not really sure, Eva. It's not really clear to me right now, but . . . it's not good.

EVA

There's no trouble that's any good! What has Earle gotten himself into, pray tell?

ADA LOU *(takes a deep breath)*

Eva . . . I really don't want to get into it this early in the morning. I don't understand it myself, but . . . Earle's . . . been discharged from the Army. And it's not an honorable discharge, either. It has something to do with another soldier . . . that I surely don't understand. It's just that Earle wouldn't say much about it. So that's all I know right now.

(EVA is too stunned to speak for a moment. She begins pacing up and down the porch.)

EVA

Not honorable? Dishonorably discharged? Well . . . he must have told you what he did. It must have been bad . . .

ADA LOU

Now, Eva, don't push me . . . Earle wouldn't talk too much about it, but he was very upset . . . very upset. He didn't feel that he could face either you or Lottie with such news. Or anybody in this town, for our sake. So, he's gone. Gone to New York City, I think.

EVA

Gone to New York City? What did he and this . . . this soldier do? Now don't talk in riddles!

ADA LOU

Eva . . . PLEASE! I DON'T KNOW!

EVA *(pacing back and forth)*

Well . . . he must'a told you something . . . they don't just throw you out of the army for some little ole thing. Did he get in a fight? *(After thought)* No, Earle's not the kind to be in a fight . . . Did he hurt somebody? I can't

199

imagine him hurting anybody.

> **ADA LOU** *(quietly and resigned)*
> Eva . . . It had something to do with . . . with sex.

(EVA suddenly stops pacing. She's startled.)

> **EVA**

Sex? Earle?

(Understanding crosses EVA's face.)
O-o-o-oh! You mean sex . . . with another man?

> **ADA LOU** *(nods yes)*
> That's as much as I know . . . as much as he told me for right now . . . and frankly I don't want to know any more.

(She starts for the front door, then lingers.)
I'm so tired . . . I'm just worn out with this funeral and all. Now this with Earle. I just want to go home . . . I want Hershal!

(She walks over and embraces EVA.)
Oh, Eva . . . I could just die! Earle . . . was so upset. It just made me sick to see how he's messed things up so. I don't know when we will see him again. It's like we just lost him along with Mama.

> **EVA** *(pats her back)*
> Don't you worry, we'll get this thing straightened out. Now, where is he? Did he really leave? I want to see him—I want to talk to him . . .

> **ADA LOU**

He left hours ago . . . on that early train to Birmingham. I don't know how to get in touch with him just now . . . he said he was going to New York City . . . so we'll just have to wait until he contacts me. He said he would.

> **EVA**

Well, I'm hurt. He should at least have said goodbye, instead of running off like some . . . some thief in the night. He didn't have to do that!

> **ADA LOU**

He didn't feel he could face you or Lottie. He wanted me to tell you. Oh, Eva, he was so hurt, so distraught! It made me feel so helpless not to be able to reach out and do something . . . but he didn't want help now.

> **EVA**

Poor soul! Oh . . . Ada Lou . . . let's not say anything about this right now to Lottie since she's leaving right after the funeral. She doesn't need any more burdens put on her right now. Oh, I know she's put on a brave front through this whole thing with Mama, but I heard her crying in the night and I don't think she's over it. *(EVA takes a handkerchief from her pocket and blows her nose.)* It's been hard on her. I think she's having some real problems with Karl. I just sense it. So there's no reason to bring it up right now. Why, she'd be on the phone to Senator Bankhead in Washington right now trying to get to the bottom of this thing. You know Lottie. So, let's not tell her until after the funeral. She'll know something when she sees he's not here. But, I'll take responsibility for that. Promise?

ADA LOU

Yes, I promise. It's probably best.

EVA

Oh, Lord . . . LORD! I just thought of something! WHAT IS AUNT EDNA GOING TO SAY ABOUT ALL THIS! OH, DAMN . . . DAMN IT TO HELL AND BACK! I swear, if she starts talking about this around town I'll go over there and snatch her bald-headed! So help me GOD!

(The screen door opens and LOTTIE steps out, still in a robe, hair in a net.)

LOTTIE

Oh, Eva . . . don't tell me you're still ranting and raving about Aunt Edna. Just forget about her, will you. She really doesn't matter now . . .

EVA *(composing herself)*

You're right . . . it doesn't matter now.

(While LOTTIE strolls the porch, EVA shakes her head violently at ADA LOU, indicating not to say a word.)

ADA LOU

Did you sleep all right?

LOTTIE

Yes . . . after a while. I must have dropped off without realizing it. I called Karl and told him I was taking the train and he seemed relieved . . . oh, he wishes he could be here, but he can't get away on such short notice. Is Earle up yet? I haven't had any time to talk with him . . . to find out what Army life is like. Where is he?

EVA

Oh . . . I think he went up to the cemetery to see if everything is going okay . . . see if ole Mose dug that grave properly. He's been doing it for a hundred years at least and I'm sure he doesn't need Earle's advice.

(She makes a face at ADA LOU and tries to change the subject.)
What time does your train leave?

LOTTIE

Oh, didn't I tell you? Ernestine Gilmer is down visiting her mother and I'm getting a ride with her as far as Memphis. Oh, I hope that child of hers doesn't get car sick. He usually does. But I'll put up with anything just to avoid having to take the train that far. I always feel that when I get to Memphis, I'm almost home.

ADA LOU *(giving LOTTIE a big hug)*

Oh, Lottie . . . I hate to see you go. I'm gonna miss you . . . and Eva. I wish you lived closer. I'd like to get to know your family better . . . and for them to know us. Especially after the war when Hershal's back. He's never met Karl.

LOTTIE

We'll do that. We'll do a lot of things after the war. I hate running off right now and leaving you and Eva to take care of getting everything settled here. I'd like to stay, but Karl is insisting that I get back. The boys are coming back from camp and he can't seem to cope with them around.

ADA LOU

Don't worry about it. I'm used to taking over now. I know I complained a lot in the past about how I wish I lived a thousand miles away from here instead of a hundred so I wouldn't have to come at the drop of a hat. But now I realize how precious that time with Mama was and I wouldn't take anything for it.

LOTTIE

Don't hesitate to write or if necessary, call me if you need help. I suppose we can't do anything about settling the estate right away. Do you think Earle wants the house? I'm sure Karl and I won't be moving down here. Florida, maybe, but not here.

ADA LOU *(concerned)*

I don't know if Earle is interested in the house at all. He never was interested in Papa's business and I'm so glad we went on and sold it. It took a lot of responsibility off Mama. And now . . . I think the best thing is to sell the house.

LOTTIE *(stares offstage)*

Who is that coming up the street?

> *(EVA and ADA LOU exchanged hurried glances, afraid that it might be Earle.)*

Oh, it's Lou Berta. I didn't realize that she came to work this early. *(Looking at her watch)* It's a quarter to six . . . does she get here at this time every day? I never noticed before. Look how slowly she moves. She's gotta be older than Mama.

EVA

I'm sure she is. She's been here forever . . . at least as long as I can remember.

LOTTIE

You know, I haven't thought about what we should do about her. We're not going to need her any more now that Mama's gone. Do we owe her any money . . . or some sort of pension?

EVA

I never heard about house help getting a pension, much less retiring.

(LOU BERTA approaches slowly, almost out of breath. She spots the flag EARLE has thrown in the bushes and picks it up.)

LOU BERTA

What's this doing out here? It belongs in the window. It's Mr. Earle's flag. Who tossed it out here in the bushes?

ADA LOU *(flustered)*

It must have been Diedre. I told her and Jimmie Ann not to be playing with that flag. My goodness . . . here . . . give it to me. I'll tend to that child.

LOTTIE

Lou Berta . . . are you going to be all right? I mean, do you have any plans . . . now that Mama's . . .

LOU BERTA

Nome . . . I haven't thought about it.

LOTTIE *(nervous)*

I sure wish I could bring you back with me to Chicago. Would you like to come?

LOU BERTA

Lawd, Miss Lottie. I ain't studying no she-car-go. No ma'm . . . it's too cold up there for me. I'm gonna stay right here until it's my time to move on. I never thought Miss Lula would go 'fore me, but I guess that the lawd hasn't prepared a place for me yet.

(LOU BERTA pauses on the steps and looks from one to the other. She is hesitant to speak, but then she talks to all, but no one specifically.)

I wants to know about Mr. Earle . . .

(ADA LOU and EVA are caught by surprise. They start to speak, but neither knows what to say.)

LOTTIE

Uhh . . . what do you mean, Lou Berta?

LOU BERTA

I mean why he was getting on that train early this morning . . . that Birmingham train . . .

LOTTIE

The train? This morning? What are you talking about?

LOU BERTA

Yes'm, that early train. Ole Skeeter down at the station asked me it this morning and I said that couldn't be Mr. Earle. His Mama is gonna be buried this morning. And he said, if it weren't him, it sho' was someone who looked just like him. Is Mr. Earle in his room?

(ADA LOU and EVA sheepishly try to avoid answering. LOTTIE looks at the both of them, suspecting something going on.)

EVA

I don't know anything about it. Not a thing!

(EVA walks to the end of the porch and turns her back on the group. ADA LOU stands trembling at the door, then turns and throws her arms around LOTTIE, sobbing.)

ADA LOU

Oh, Lottie . . . Earle's in some awful trouble . . . just awful.

(LOTTIE and LOU BERTA exchange worried glances.)

LOTTIE

Tell me about it . . . start at the beginning.

ACT TWO

SCENE THREE

(LOTTIE stands on the porch, a suitcase at her side, looking at her watch from time to time. She paces a few steps, then turns around as Lou Berta comes through door still dressed in funeral wear.)

LOTTIE *(handing her an envelope)*

Lou Berta, I want you to have this. At least it's something for right now.

LOU BERTA *(reluctantly stuffs it in a pocket)*

I thank you Miss Lottie, but there's no need to do that.

LOTTIE

It's just a little token until we get things settled. I don't know anything about Mama's will, but I am sure there's something in there for you. My god, you're one of the family.

(LOTTIE almost begins to cry, but gains composure.)

Every time I thought about Mama . . . and home, you were right there in my thoughts, too. *(Gives a little laugh)* Remember when I was in the first grade my teacher, Miss Cousins I think it was, asked me what my mother's name was and I said, "Lou Berta." *(Laughs)* Oh, was she shocked! I can't imagine her not seeing the humor in that, but I remember she stopped by after school and had a little talk with Mama about it . . .

LOU BERTA *(chuckling to herself)*

Lord, yes! I remember that . . . but Miss Lula put her straight. She sho' didn't like me for some reason. Like that time on the train when I was taking you up to yo' Aunt Mamie's. We were sitting in the white folks car and she didn't see you with me, and she got up and came over to say something . . . and . . . (*Chuckles*) and then she saw you and she just kept on-n-n-n going out of that car! I know'd she was gonna say some'm, but I had the last laugh. But you couldn't ride in the colored car. The conductor wouldn't have stood for it. So, I got to ride all the way to Birmingham in the white folks car! And I laughed all the way. Ummm-hmmmm!

LOTTIE

I remember us being together on the train, but I don't remember Miss Cousins being there. Funny . . . so many things I've forgotten. Especially about this house. Oh, I was always in such a hurry to run off from here . . . to someplace I thought was more exciting . . . more adventurous. Then when the day came to leave, I didn't want to go. And you were no help!

(*LOTTIE throws her arm around LOU BERTA's shoulder.*)

. . . You would always come out with some gorgeous Strawberry Shortcake, or something to break my heart and make me homesick before I even started out! Ahh . . . I would sit there on the back porch eating it, choking back tears, wanting to stay, but afraid not to go after making such a to-do about going off.

LOU BERTA

You had itchy feet, Miss Lottie. They ain't no cure for that. You just gotta go until they stop itching, then you'll be okay. Has they?

LOTTIE

Has what?

LOU BERTA

Stopped itching? Yo' feet.

(*LOTTIE gives it a lot of thought. She walks over to the porch rail and looks out.*)

LOTTIE

I'd say . . . yes. There's no place I want to run to any more. Not like when I was young. I've "settled down" as they say . . . but there are some things I would like to change. Yes, some things. And I think they will . . . for the most part. They're changing now. (*Reflects*) Maybe one of the good things about getting older is that we're much more able to understand things for what they are . . . and that it's sometimes easier to stand and fight for what you want, rather than to run away and seek a new starting point.

(*LOTTIE walks slowly up the porch.*)

Talking about new starts, I'm just sick over Earle. Just sick. I've got a call into Senator Bankhead's office. Papa help put him in office, so he can surely look into this matter. I just don't understand how they can throw him out for . . . for . . . whatever.

LOU BERTA

Ummmm-hummm. Yes'm, it don't sound right. That po' child. He's gonna do a lot of running 'fore it's over, and it ain't from itchy feet.

LOTTIE

I've had some experience in these things . . . especially when I went to Columbia, but I just can't associate them with Earle. He doesn't seem the type . . . I mean, the people I met that were . . . well, arty-types, you know, were in theatre . . . or into dance. Earle just doesn't seem to fit that mold in my mind. Oh, I wish I could have talked to him before he went off.

LOU BERTA

Yes'm . . . I don't like him going off like that a'tall. I thought something was wrong last night . . . that he wasn't acting hisself. I could tell he was up to something. But I ain't worried about him. Not about Mr. Sam's boy. He'll come through this OK, I know that. May take a while, but he'll sort it out. So, don't you worry 'bout him, Miss Lottie. He'll find a way . . . sooner or later.

LOTTIE

Oh, I do hope so. I always pictured Earle settling down here . . . taking over this house . . . and keeping the family centered here. But when he was adamant about not wanting to take over the store, maybe he knew something then about not setting up a life here. I just don't know.

(The door swings open and ADA LOU comes out on the porch.)

ADA LOU

Have any of you seen Dee? I don't want her running over to Francis Evelyn's house this afternoon. I want her to stay here. I think the funeral really upset her and I'm not so sure it was the right thing to let her attend.

LOTTIE

Of course it was, Ada Lou. You can't shield children from death. They have to learn sometime. I remember seeing Grandma Molloy laid out right here in the living room and I don't think it got me all disturbed at all. In fact I found it fascinating with all the people coming and going and eating out on the porch. Oh, Lord, remember how it was a virtual feast laid out in the dining room? It was enough food to feed an army.

ADA LOU

Well . . . there's enough in there now to feed us for days. Did Eva pack you a little something to eat on the train? The fried chicken is OK, but I told here not to pack any of those deviled eggs, or any of that congealed stuff that won't keep . . .

(Door swings open and EVA comes out with a large paper bag.)

EVA

We're almost out of waxed paper, but I think this will keep until you get on the train. Oh, I wish you could take some of that pie that Julia Reedy made . . . but I put in some of her dinner rolls. Oh, they are heaven! She won't tell anybody her recipe, but I'd swear she uses beer instead of yeast . . . and she couldn't tell that. Not up at the church. (*Somewhat to herself*) I wonder where she gets the beer in this town? Humm-m-m-m. Oh, Lottie, I couldn't find that ole thermos so you could have some ice tea. You'll just have to buy a co-cola on the train.

LOTTIE

Oh, I don't need a thermos. They always have something cold to drink on the train.

(A calm falls over the group as though no one can think of anything else to say. It is a sad time, a parting, and this time it is especially sad because it ends an era. The ladies move in different directions, lost in their own thoughts, reluctant to speak.)

LOTTIE

I have this strange feeling that this is the last time I will be standing on this porch . . . It's scary, but somehow I know it's true. Maybe it's just as well, because I don't think I can handle seeing strangers sitting out here instead of family . . . and not being able to just walk up the steps and find Mama in the parlor . . . and go up to my old room and plop down. I got over Papa not being here, but Mama? *(Snaps out of it)* Oh, where is Miz Gilmer . . . you can't depend on those train schedules any more . . .

EVA

Well, there's no reason for me to come back here. What am I going to do? Sit on the porch and jaw with Aunt Edna? Mercy! Can't you just see that.

ADA LOU

She was very nice to all of us at the service . . . you gotta give her credit for that. I think she's trying to make up for things. I noticed that she even took the very back family pew . . . and she didn't say one word about Earle not being there. Nobody did.

EVA

Everybody knows, that's why. No wonder Mr. Wheeler fought so hard to get on the draft board when no else wanted it. It put him in line to know everything about everybody's business in regards to the war. I remember something Papa said about him not going to the first World War. I wish I could remember what it was, because it might shut him up about Earle. I know Aunt Edna knows it since she knows everything in this town, but I'm not about to ask her.

ADA LOU

I think for once, Aunt Edna may be deeply embarrassed about all this. After all, Earle is her nephew and this is something you just don't gossip about casually.

EVA

Well, it didn't stop her ruining my reputation . . . or trying to. You know, I still want to go over there and get this settled once and for all before I leave . . .

LOTTIE

You'll do nothing of the kind! And Eva . . . no Lou Berta . . . don't you dare go down there to Dr. Strawbridge's Drug store and bring back any of that . . . that VILE stuff. I don't want to even hear about a repeat scene of that nature! Whew! My head still hurts!

(Sound of car horn)

Oh . . . there's Miz Gilmer. Yoo-hoo!

(She waves off stage. Again there is a moment of hesitation. The three sisters converge and embrace as one.)

Take care, and Ada Lou, call me if you need me.

(LOTTIE breaks away for a long embrace with EVA alone. Then she turns to LOU BERTA for a similar embrace as DIEDRE races out the door.)

DIEDRE

Aunt Lottie, Aunt Lottie!

(DIEDRE hugs her around the waist.)

When are you gonna bring Karl Jr. and Stephen down to play with me? When?

LOTTIE

Oh, as soon as I can, Dee. Soon . . . Be a good girl, you hear?

(Gives DIEDRE a hug and kiss.)

Now mind your Mama . . . and make your daddy proud.

DIEDRE

Yes m'am. I will.

(LOTTIE takes a last look around and then hurriedly leaves. The slam of a car door and a toot of the horn as the car she is in pulls away. All parties assume positions around the porch. ADA LOU sits on the steps and DIEDRE comes and sits beside her.)

DIEDRE

Did Mam-Ma go right to Heaven? . . . I mean, how do you just go to Heaven?

ADA LOU

Honey, I don't really know how it's done, it just happens. When you're a good person like your Mam-Ma . . . you just go straight to Heaven.

DIEDRE

Do all soldiers go straight to heaven if they die? Even if they're Germans

208

and Japs?

ADA LOU

I suppose so . . . if they were good.

DIEDRE

Would Daddy go straight to Heaven if he got killed?

LOU BERTA *(jumping to the occasion)*

Come here, child, I got some lemonade back in the kitchen for you . . .

DIEDRE

But would he, Mama? Would he?

(ADA LOU puts her arm around DIEDRE and draws her near.)

ADA LOU

Yes, I'm sure he would, but don't think things like that. Your Daddy is gonna come home when all this is over. So, keep thinking that . . . and keep writing him . . . every week.

(EVA, with tears in her eyes, has been watching this touching scene with mother and child thinking, perhaps, of her lost daughter. EVA walks to one end of the porch, speaking to no one in particular.)

EVA

It's always so sad when someone leaves, isn't it? Even if you're together for just a short while, it's like a part of you breaks off when someone goes off. Mama used to say it was unbearable when any of us came and stayed a while and then left. It was like she counted the minutes until the next visit. Almost like the clock stopped until that moment of return. Oh, it must have been lonely here all by herself. I even get lonely when Morris goes off on the road. At least I have someone to shout at instead of the radio.

(EVA lights another cigarette, not caring who sees her.)

ADA LOU

Eva! You shouldn't be smoking out here. Someone may see you!

EVA

Oh, I don't care any more. Why should I? I don't care about this town . . . this house . . . or what anyone one, especially Aunt Edna . . . thinks about me, or what I do. It's all changed now . . . the end of our family. Now Aunt Edna can revel in her righteousness since she has won the war with us Nolans! Her decadent foes have now been scattered to the ends of the earth. Lottie's not coming back here. I know that. And certainly not Earle. So that just leaves you and me and I sure am not going to be running off up here any more. *(Starts to cry.)* Oh, if I could have had just one more moment with Mama . . . just one more moment!

ADA LOU

Eva . . . don't do that to yourself. Here . . . come here and sit down by me.

209

(EVA reluctantly goes over and sits on the steps.)

We can't just let things fall apart. We're still family. Oh, there's going to be some adjusting to do, but we can handle it. Already I feel much better about Earle. Just letting a little time pass between things can make a difference. He's still Earle, no matter what other people, especially what people here might think. Nothing stays the same. You know that. Things are always changing and not necessarily for the worse. It may seem that way at first, but I've been learning to keep thinking good thoughts . . . good thoughts for Earle . . . and you . . . and Lottie . . . and Lou Berta, all of us. And I know deep down that those good things are going to be better than anything we have ever experienced before.

EVA *(rises and walks toward end of porch)*

Well, I certainly hope you're right. I need some good things happening for me. I sure do. I know Morris and I certainly have some things to work out. *(EVA registers a thought.)* Maybe I should get involved in the war effort? It just came to me. I've got lots of time . . . now that I don't have to worry about Mama. Maybe I should volunteer down at the USO. I've been asked to play the piano down there and help entertain.

(EVA gets a somewhat devilish look on her face.)

Mobile is overrun now with sailors . . . and soldiers . . . they do need volunteers.

(EVA turns to ADA LOU for approval.)

You don't think . . . you don't think that it's kinda "fast" on my part, do you? I mean, everybody's doing something for the war effort.

ADA LOU

I think you should look into it right away.

EVA

You do? Well . . . I just might. Yes, I just might do it. *(A smile crosses her face.)* Yes, I am gonna do it!

(EVA heads inside with a spring to her step as she anticipates a new start about to happen.)

LOU BERTA *(turns and heads for the door)*

Miss Ada Lou, I'm gonna put some of that food away 'fore it gets spoiled. They's plenty to eat here tonight . . .

ADA LOU

You're so right. *(With a resigned sigh)* You know . . . I think I'll make up a plate to take over to Aunt Edna's. There's no sense in letting all that food go to waste. For the family's sake, maybe we need to make a little peace offering.

LOU BERTA

That sho' would be nice, Miss Ada Lou. It sho' would. You is truly Miss

Lula's girl, you know that, don't you? You take after her the most, and she said to me not long ago how much she counted on you and how she was 'fraid she asked too much of you. But I tell you now, she was mighty proud of her Ada Lou . . . and I know Miss Lula is smiling down on you right now . . . Yes'm I do.

(ADA LOU is a bit too embarrassed to acknowledge the compliment, but she is more than pleased at the remarks.)

ADA LOU

Thank you, Lou Berta . . . thank you. Come on, Dee. You make up a plate for Jimmie Ann and I'll do one for Francis Evelyn and Aunt Edna. We'd better hurry before they start supper.

(ADA LOU and DIEDRE enter the house and LOU BERTA lingers on the, porch, looking up at the sky. LOU BERTA walks a little way down the porch, humming some spiritual, and picks up a fan from a chair and fans herself. She looks up to the sky, craning her neck upward and looking all around.)

LOU BERTA

Them children are gonna be all right, Miss Lula. Ain't gonna be easy, I know that . . . They gonna be all-right . . . you wait and see! *(To herself and no one in particular)* Ummm-hummm . . . looks like tomorrow's gonna be another scorcher . . .

(LOU BERTA continues to pace the porch slowly, humming and fanning herself.)

Yes'm, gonna be all-right . . .

CURTAIN

APPENDIX I

Guidelines for Entering the Competition

Winning scripts are produced in New York by The Open Book under the Actors Equity Showcase Code. Playwrights receive contracts conforming to Dramatists Guild standards. Separate negotiations are conducted in case of publication.

Scripts may be drama, prose and/or poetry. Entries do not have to be in readers theatre format, but winning entries may require adaptation or permission to adapt. Entries must not have been produced professionally within a one hundred mile radius of New York City or within 18 months of the closing date of the contest.

Adaptations are acceptable if source material is in the public domain, or if a copy of a permission license is included. Do not send scripts which merely arrange adapted material for oral interpretation. To vie with original plays submitted by other writers, adaptations must be brilliantly-realized readers theatre scripts like Charles LaBorde's 1994 winner, *Memorial*.

Do not submit scripts with elaborate lighting or sets, unless they can be simplified. Plays requiring multiple settings probably will not be selected.

Smoking is unacceptable; scripts chosen for production must be cut or rewritten to eliminate onstage smoking.

Sound effects and music are permissible. Scripts may include *a capella* or piano music.

Do not submit scripts requiring more than nine characters—and be aware that small casts (from one to six performers) *are strongly preferred*. Good parts for women are especially appreciated. Scripts cannot require child actors or onstage animals. *IMPORTANT: In keeping with equal employment policy promulgated by Actors Equity Association (as well as readers theatre convention), The Open Book reserves the right to cast nontraditionally with regard to age, race and gender.* Maximum playing time: two hours *with one intermission*. One-act plays are acceptable.

Scripts must be single-side typed on white paper. *Include a list of characters immediately after the title page.*

Send one copy of each entry with a handling fee of ten dollars ($10.00) *for each entry* by December 1 to:

> The Open Book
> 525 West End Ave., Suite 12-E
> New York NY 10024-3207

Make checks or money orders to "The Open Book." *NO CASH!* Fees are tax-deductible to the full extent permitted by law.

If you wish script(s) returned, enclose a self-addressed stamped envelope. (Make certain that the envelope is big enough!) If you want to be sure that your script was received, enclose a self-addressed stamped postcard.

Include a brief biographical sketch. If applicable, enclose a production history, reviews, programs.

NOTE: The competition will be held annually till further notice.6

---

6   Within reason, of course. Query if this book is more than a few years old, and don't forget to include a self-addressed, stamped envelope for the reply.

APPENDIX II

Songs Used in The Open Book Production of *Memorial*

Special material was written by Marvin Kaye for the New York premiere of *Memorial.* The opening was staged to a march with each couplet spoken in turn by nine performers. "Body count" and the cadence was spoken, respectively, by an "officer" and the "noncom" D. I. The second line of each chorus was chanted, first by three, then six and finally by all nine actors. The last line was sung.

A license to use this material may be obtained from The Open Book upon formal application and payment of a $10.00 honorarium to **The Open Book, 525 West End Avenue, Suite 12 E, New York NY, 10024-3207.**

1. Opening Sequence

SOLDIERS (marching)
Don't blame us. France came first.
We got there later and we got the worst.
Don't blame us. Don't look back
Especially after a napalm attack.
Don't blame us. Fight all night.
Pray to God and shoot on sight.
Body count—hut two, hut two—
Kill the Cong or they'll kill you.
Don't blame me. Not my fault.
I didn't hear the major when he hollered "halt."
Don't blame me. I'm just a kid.
I fire my rifle and don't give a shit.
 Not my fault. Don't blame me.
We only followed orders, man, now don't you see?
 Body count—two three four—
Why did we fight this mother-fuckin' war?
Don't forget. For the flag
I changed my khaki for a body bag.
Now don't forget. I was there.
Didn't run to Canada with fruitcake hair.
Don't forget. I survived.
But nobody gave a damn when I arrived.

215

Body count—hut two three
(Sung) For the home of the brave, and the land of the free.

2. Protest Sequence

(A group of protesters step forward and sing.)
PROTESTERS (to tune of Alexander's Ragtime Band)
Come on along, come on along,
Come on and fight for Uncle Sam!
He's callin' me, he's callin' you
To join the boys in Vietnam.
You will hear a bugle call like you never heard before
And every goddamn morning you are gonna hear some more.
We're the greatest Army Corps that am—
In Vietnam!
You'll get a gun, a great big gun,
And a hand grenade or two.
We'll make 'em run, and when we're done,
They will learn a thing or two.
'cause we're gonna kick some yella ass down the Mekong River
For Uncle Sam, for Uncle Sam—
We're the boys of Vietnam.
(A second group of protesters replaces the first.)
NEW PROTESTERS (to tune of The Caisson Song)
Every bush, every tree
Hides another enemy
But they won't be behind them for long
Mow 'em down, mow 'em down
We will march into their town
'cause we're going to mop up the Cong.
And it's two—three—four
Why do we fight this war?
The general, he never told us why.
But who gives a damn?
We'll die in Vietnam
And we'll a-all join Jesus in the sky!

216

APPENDIX III

Other Recommended Scripts

Second place was a tie between Jo Davidsmeyer's *Angel*, published in this volume, and Elizabeth Hemmerdinger's *Star Dust*, a two-character drama about a distaff TV personality and an unbalanced young woman stalking her. A play that could easily be adapted to readers theatre, *Star Dust* has a plot that at first seems familiar, though fascinating, but the playwright avoids the expected with an engrossing series of psychological twists that are at turns sad, funny, chilling, and—most wonderful of all—ultimately deeply moving. For details about this script, contact: **Elizabeth Hemmerdinger, 40 Central Park South, New York NY, 10019.**

The following plays reached the semifinal round in the First National Readers Theatre Competition. Though written as conventional theatre scripts, all are capable of being adapted to readers theatre.

Bittersweet by Rose Ann Kalister is a comedy-drama about a Syrian family learning to cope with their aging mother suffering from Alzheimer's Disease. Excellent roles for four men and four women, especially the clan's ailing matriarch. For details about this script, contact: **Rose Ann Kalister, 1133 Upland Drive, Columbus, Ohio, 43229.**

Hanley's World by Arthur Winslow is a comedy about a TV talk show that in its quest for ratings books a man who says he is Satan and a young woman who claims she is the Christ. The two square off in a witty and provocative verbal battle that builds to a startling climax. Three women, two men, one interior. For details about this script, contact: **Arthur Winslow, # 1 Vienna Drive, Santa Ana, California, 92703.**

Jane Austen Never Slept Here is subtitled "An Emotional Striptease for four women and one man." Its authors, Laurie Rae Dietrich, Helen Merino, and Heidi Decker, who devised it for the InYourFace Theatre Company of San Antonio, Texas, describe it as "a performance at an emotional strip club. The strippers bare their souls, instead of their skin." The "strippers" tell all about their romantic (and not-so ditto) relationships. A bare stage and stools are the minimal production requirements. For details about this script, contact: **The Open Book, 525 West End Avenue, Suite 12 E, New York NY, 10024-3207.**

Mequasset by the Sea by Jolene Goldenthal is about five women, childhood friends, who meet on a midsummer day at a quiet New England beach, a place that holds poignant memories for each. All roles provide excellent material for character actresses. For details, contact: **Helen Merrill, 435 West 23 Street, New York NY, 10011.**

Muckraker by Russell Whaley is the true story of Gaston B. Means, a major figure in the scandals surrounding U. S. President Warren Harding. Based on published information and conversations, the play speculates on the First Lady's involvement in her husband's death. Roles for five men and four women, with a single interior that can suggest several locations. For details, contact: **The Open Book, 525 West End Avenue, Suite 12 E, New York NY, 10024-3207.**

Night Out by Dan Remmes is a romantic comedy about a man who tries to win back a woman he abandoned four years ago. The setting is a suite at New York's posh St. Moritz Hotel. Two main characters plus a bellhop—a delightful comic cameo. For details, contact: **The Open Book, 525 West End Avenue, Suite 12 E, New York NY, 10024-3207.**

The Orchard by Caroline E. Wood is a romantic one-act drama for one man and two women, an excellent companion piece to the author's *The Immigrant Garden*. For details about this script, contact: **Caroline E. Wood, 6316 Willow Grove, Longview WA, 98632.**

The Rest Stop by Gloria Martin Shoemaker is a poignant one-act comedy-drama set in a bed and board care home for the aged. Excellent parts for five women (one nonspeaking role). The Open Book produced *The Rest Stop* as a curtain-raiser to Caroline Wood's *The Immigrant Garden*. For details, contact: **The Open Book, 525 West End Avenue, Suite 12 E, New York NY, 10024-3207.**

Waiting by Elyse Nass deals with an estranged family brought together in a hospital waiting room to face a crisis. The individuals are each forced to examine their responsibility to family, as well as secrets of childhood, self-determination and the difficult need to forgive. No technical requirements; minimal set and props; roles for one man and two women. For details, contact: **Elyse Nass, 59-15 47th Avenue, Woodside NY, 11377.**

Walls and Bridges by Bruce E. Massis is the story of four military nurses stationed in Vietnam who return after the war with their therapist to face their demons and seek closure to that part of their lives. Excellent roles for five women, simple set requirements. For details, contact: **Bruce E. Massis, 120 West 73 Street, Apartment B, New York NY, 10023.**